MALACHI

BHHB

Baylor Handbook on the Hebrew Bible

General Editor

W. Dennis Tucker Jr.

$35.80

DISCARDED

MALACHI
A Handbook on the Hebrew Text

Terry W. Eddinger

BAYLOR UNIVERSITY PRESS

Shelton State Libraries
Shelton State Community College

© 2012 by Baylor University Press, Waco, Texas 76798

All Rights Reserved. No part of this publication may be reproduced, stored in a retrieval system, or transmitted, in any form or by any means, electronic, mechanical, photocopying, recording or otherwise, without the prior permission in writing of Baylor University Press.

Cover Design by Pamela Poll
Cover photograph by Bruce and Kenneth Zuckerman, West Semitic Research, in collaboration with the Ancient Biblical Manuscript Center. Courtesy Russian National Library (Saltykov-Shchedrin).

Library of Congress Cataloging-in-Publication Data

Eddinger, Terry.
  Malachi : a handbook on the Hebrew text / Terry W. Eddinger.
  174 p. cm. -- (Baylor handbook on the Hebrew Bible)
  Includes bibliographical references and index.
  ISBN 978-1-60258-427-3 (pbk. : alk. paper)
  1. Bible. O.T. Malachi--Language, style. 2. Bible. O.T. Malachi--Criticism, Textual. 3. Hebrew language--Grammar. 4. Hebrew language--Discourse analysis. I. Title.
  BS1675.55.E33 2012
  224'.990446--dc23
                          2011051771

BAYLOR ®
UNIVERSITY

Printed in the United States of America on acid-free paper with a minimum of 30% pcw recycled content.

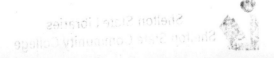

In honor of my Biblical Hebrew professors in seminary

Albert F. Bean
Joel F. Drinkard, Jr.
M. Pierce Matheney, Jr.
Thomas G. Smothers
John D. W. Watts

And in memory of and humble gratitude to

Page H. Kelley

Whose love for Biblical Hebrew rivaled only his love for God.

TABLE OF CONTENTS

ACKNOWLEDGMENTS

As a Ph.D. student, I translated Malachi for the first time many years ago. I found the book very interesting, both in terms of the straightforward language of the text and in the artistry the prophet uses in delivering his message. I was intrigued by his extensive use of the question and answer pseudo-dialogue, a method other prophets used sparsely. This, and his blending of poetic elements into the prose of the text, made the text fun and exciting to translate. I hope persons who use this handbook to assist them in translating the book of Malachi find the same joy and excitement I did.

I would like to express my appreciation to the faculty and administration of Carolina Graduate School of Divinity for their support and encouragement while I worked on this project. Their kind words and prayers meant much to me. Also, I would like to thank my Hebrew students who have learned to love the language as I do and who often expressed how they were looking forward to seeing this work in print. May they find this work useful as they become the next generation of Hebrew scholars. Particularly, I want to thank Dr. James Wagner for reading my manuscript and offering helpful suggestions and corrections. Through many conversations, Dr. Wagner helped me determine the approach and shape of this work.

I wish to thank the good people at *BibleWorks* whose computer program assisted me in creating the Hebrew word chart found in the appendix. The efficiency of their *BibleWorks* program really sped up the process of creating the chart, as it made seeing the occurrences of Hebrew words in Malachi very easy.

The team at Baylor University Press has been a pleasure to work with during this process. They have been most helpful in seeing this book to fruition. Specifically, I am very grateful to Dr. W. Dennis Tucker Jr., the Baylor Handbook of the Hebrew Bible series editor, for the opportunity to write this handbook. Also, his careful review of my text and sage advice led to a much better and more complete manuscript.

Finally, I wish to thank my mom and dad who have always encouraged me in my many undertakings. I wish to thank my wife Cynthia who has encouraged me during this project and supported me at every level, making sacrifices so that I could devote time to writing it. Also, I would like to thank my young son Hunter, who often visited me in my home office and asked, "How is Malachi coming?" Precious are such words of encouragement from a caring young heart and mind. Thanks to all of you for your love and support.

Terry W. Eddinger

ABBREVIATIONS

abs	absolute
AC	Bill Arnold and John H. Choi, *A Guide to Biblical Hebrew Syntax.* Cambridge: Cambridge University Press, 2003
act	active
adv	adverb
advers	adversative
art	article
BDB	Francis I. Brown, with S. R. Driver, and Charles A. Briggs, *A Hebrew and English Lexicon of the Old Testament.* Oxford: Clarendon, 1907
BHS	K. Elliger and W. Ruldolf, *Biblica Hebraica Stuttgartensia.* Stuttgart: Deutsche Bibelgesellschaft, 1984
c	common
cf.	compare
chs	chapters
CHAL	William L. Holladay, ed., *A Concise Hebrew and Aramaic Lexicon of the Old Testament.* Grand Rapids: Eerdmans, 1988
coll	collective
conj	conjunction
consec	consecutive
constr	construct
cop	copulative
def	definite
demons	demonstrative

dir obj	direct object
f	feminine
GKC	Emil Kautzsch, ed., *Gesenius' Hebrew Grammar*. Translated and revised by A. E. Cowley. 2nd Engl. ed. Oxford: Clarendon, 1910
GM	Beth Glazier-McDonald, *Malachi: The Divine Messenger*. SBL Dissertation Series 98. Atlanta: Scholars, 1987
HALOT	Ludwig Koehler and Walter Baumgartner, *The Hebrew and Aramaic Lexicon of the Old Testament*. 2 vols. Revised by Walter Baumgartner and Johann Jakob Stamm. Translated by M. E. J. Richardson. Leiden, The Netherlands: Brill, 2001
Hiph	Hiphil
Hoph	Hophal
hypoth	hypothetical
ICC	John Merlin Powis Smith, *A Critical and Exegetical Commentary on Haggai, Zechariah, Malachi, and Jonah*. In Hinckley G. Mitchell, John M. P. Smith, and Julius A. Bewer, The International Critical Commentary. Edinburgh: T&T Clark, 1912
impv	imperative
indep	independent
indir obj	indirect object
inf	infinitive
interj	interjection
interrog	interrogative
jus	jussive
KD	C. F. Keil, "Malachi." In *Commentary on the Old Testament*. Vol 10: *Minor Prophets*. C. F. Keil and F. Delitzsch, eds. Edinburgh: T&T Clark, 1891. Repr. Peabody, Mass.: Hendrickson, 1996
LXX	Greek Septuagint
m	masculine

MNK	Christo H. J. van der Merwe, Jackie A. Naudé, and Jan H. Kroeze, *A Biblical Hebrew Reference Grammar*. Biblical Languages: Hebrew 3. New York: Sheffield Academic Press; Continuum, 2006
neg	negative
NIDOT	Willem A. VanGemeren, ed., *New International Dictionary of Old Testament Theology & Exegesis*. 5 vols. Grand Rapids: Zondervan, 1997
Niph	Niphal
obj	object
part	particle
pass	passive
pers	personal
Pi	Piel
pl	plural
pr	proper
prep	preposition
pron	pronoun
ptc	participle
Pu	Pual
rel	relative
s	singular
suf	suffix
subj	subject
subst	substantive
TDOT	G. Johannes Botterweck, *Theological Dictionary of the Old Testament*. Edited by Johannes Botterweck, Helmer Ringgren, and Heinz-Josef Fabry. Translated by John T. Willis and David E. Green. 15 vols. Grand Rapids: Eerdmans, 1974–2006
temp	temporal
vss	verses
WO	Bruce K. Waltke and Michael O'Connor, *An Introduction to Biblical Hebrew Syntax*. Winona Lake, Ind.: Eisenbrauns, 1990

INTRODUCTION

The book of Malachi has a simplistic and straightforward style of Biblical Hebrew at a moderate level of translating difficulty. Scholars agree on the unity of the text and the language is clear. These make Malachi a good book for a second-year Biblical Hebrew student to translate. The purpose of this handbook is aid the student or translator in the translation process, especially to assist with grammar and syntax.

Biblical Hebrew students learn basic grammar, how to parse words, and how to translate sentences in their Hebrew introductory classes. Translating Biblical Hebrew, however, is much more than just looking up words in a lexicon. Words function within larger structures—in clauses, sentences, and paragraphs—therefore, meaning is tied to understanding the broader context. Although I include much of the basic elements of Biblical Hebrew grammar in this work, I tried to provide more than what a student can find in a lexicon or basic grammar; that is, I show how words and phrases function in clauses and sentences. By looking at these larger blocks of text, one will find richer meaning in the message of the text. This book is designed to be used in the initial stage of working with the Hebrew text and does not attempt to replace the second step of consulting commentaries and secondary literature, works that deal with broader interpretation and theological issues. Now, let us turn our attention to structural and literary issues for the book of Malachi.

Structure

The prophet's message is for a post-exilic Jewish community and takes the form of oracles. These oracles can be easily divided, exposing a clear literary structure. Scholars generally agree that the structure of the book of Malachi is as follows:

Superscription, 1:1
First Oracle, 1:2-5
Second Oracle, 1:6–2:9
Third Oracle, 2:10-16
Fourth Oracle, 2:17–3:5
Fifth Oracle, 3:6-12
Sixth Oracle, 3:13-21
Two Appendices, 3:22, 3:23-24

For a discussion on the divisions of oracles, see Hill, 26; Stuart, 1249, 1263; Glazier-McDonald, 19; Smith, 299; Redditt, 152–53; and others. I follow this structure in this handbook. Verhoef, and a few other scholars, differ on their view of the book's structure. They add another pericope by dividing the second oracle into two parts: 1:6-14 and 2:1-9 (Verhoef, 171). Kaiser follows Verhoef except he combines 2:1-9 and 10-16 into one section and makes 2:17–3:12 one section (Kaiser, 17–18), with the result of five oracles rather than six. Note that the chapter breaks in Hebrew and English Bibles do not follow literary divisions and are of little help in determining the book's structure. *BHS* offers only three pericopes: 1:1–2:9; 2:10-12; and 2:13–3:21; and the appendix 3:22-24. These divisions fail to take into account the oracular structure and natural literary divisions of the book and are not helpful in determining literary structure. For more information on the Masoretic divisions of the Hebrew text of Malachi, see Hill, 26–27.

Scholars widely hold to the unity of the Masoretic Text of Malachi (Merrill, 381). They generally agree, however, that 3:22-24 are later additions either to soften the text or to provide an appropriate ending to the book, the Book of the Twelve, or to the Hebrew Bible. The only other verses seriously questioned as to being original to the text are 2:7 and 2:11-13a (see *BHS* notes 7[a], 11/12 [c–c], 13[a–a]); however, the evidence is not compelling that these verses are additions (see ICC, 4; Merrill, 381; contra Eissfeldt, 442). For more information on these additions, see discussion on each text below.

Literary Forms and Devices

Scholars generally agree that the Hebrew Bible is written in two literary styles—poetry and prose. Poetry often has parallelism, word pairs, and artistic and figurative language. Prose is often straightforward narrative, as in telling a story. Malachi is not clearly either one; therefore, scholars disagree as to its literary style. Hill lays out a good overview of scholars' positions but concludes Malachi is oracular prose (see Hill, 23–26), as do many English speaking scholars (Smith, 301). Glazier-McDonald and many German scholars argue that the book is poetic (see GM, 3–6; Smith, 301), using a broad view of the definition of poetry. Scholars tend to follow one of these two positions. However, I prefer a third position. I think the writer combines the two literally styles to create a hybrid, a blend of poetry and prose creating a poetic prose. The book reads as a conversation in a prosaic discourse with little regard for line length as usually found in poetry. However, the text is highly stylized, using all the elements of poetry—parallelism (synonymous and antithetical), word pairs, figurative language (including hyperbole), chiasms, and artistic language. The text is a true hybrid, perhaps the best example of such in the Hebrew Bible.

In the book of Malachi, the major literary device is prophetic disputation, a form of lawsuit where two or more parties, in this case, Yahweh, the priests, and the people, are at odds (Tate, 391). These disputations are presented in the form of oracles. Hortatory style is the predominate literary form and is found in all but two verses (1:1 and 3:16). Of the 53 verses in this style, 47 have Yahweh speaking in first person (Hill, 38). These verses occasionally have narrative

injections, with the most popular ones being the messenger formula
(אָמַר יְהוָה צְבָאוֹת) and cues marking a change in speaker (or pseudo-
speaker). Verses 1:1 and 3:16 are in narrative discourse entirely.

The writer prefers using rhetorical pseudo-dialogue in the format
of questions and answers to introduce and delineate Yahweh's issues
with the priests and the people of Judah. Some scholars call this style
"Socratic" or "catechetical," meaning that it is a teaching format
(Smith, 300). Although no prophet uses the question and answer format to the extent Malachi does, this style is not unique to Malachi.
Micah uses questions in his message to Judah (1:5; 2:6-11; 6:6-11)
as do Isaiah (40:12-17, 28-31), Jeremiah (2:5-8), Ezekiel (12:21-28),
Amos (8:1-2), Zechariah (chs. 1–8), and others. Petersen points out
that Malachi's didactic question and answer format is similar to the
ancient Greek diatribe, where the primary speaker quotes a secondary
party using short, highly stylized, nonverbatim discourse that is often
hyperbolic (Petersen, 31).

Merrill points out that much of the catechetical dialogue within
the oracles has a three-part common structure—assertion, objection,
and response (Merrill, 383; Wendland, 112). A discourse begins with
Yahweh making an assertion, that is, a statement of fact (as in 1:6a),
followed by an objection in the form of a rhetorical question from the
audience (as in 1:6b), and then Yahweh responding to the question
(as in 1:6c).

The prophet places a strong emphasis upon and draws authority from the Mosaic covenant. Therefore, the translator should pay
attention to the writer's use of covenant language, which is preva-
lent throughout the book. Words such as אָהֵב "love," יְרֵא "fear,"
בְּרֵךְ "blessing," אָרַר "curse," בְּרִית "covenant," and תּוֹרָה "instruction" appear regularly in Malachi and occur frequently in Deuteronomy and in the Deuteronomistic History. In the Pentateuch, these
words have a strong association with the covenant and this allusion
is intended in Malachi. Certainly, the prophet wanted to connect his
message to the priests and the people of Judah with the covenant and

have it supported by covenantal authority. See Stuart, 1257–62 for more information on Malachi's use of Deuteronomistic language.

Using this Handbook

This handbook is intended to aid in translation of the Hebrew text to English but it is not a commentary on the text. I have not included background material typically found in a commentary such as dating, authorship, and setting, and I do not discuss the theological implications one might glean from a passage. A number of commentaries do a tremendous job at discussing these issues and students should consult them for this information. My focus is on understanding the text itself. However, I do discuss textual variants, such as those listed in the textual apparatus of *Biblica Hebraica Stuttgartensia*, as these readings affect the translation of the text.

I have included a translation of the text at the beginning of each pericope. I discuss significant elements for each pericope before beginning a verse-by-verse discussion of the text. This includes a brief discussion of the format of the text itself, usually an oracle, and a chart of key words in the section. The key word charts list words that have significant meaning for the text. Under the discussion of each verse, I break down the text further into clauses and phrases, and in some cases, individual words. I parse all of the verbs and discuss how each element (verbs, nouns, adjectives, etc.) functions within the text. The Appendix contains a list of all the Hebrew words found in Malachi along with the chapter and verse references for each occurrence. A glossary of terms is located at the back of the book with basic definitions of terms commonly used throughout this handbook.

A HANDBOOK ON THE HEBREW TEXT OF MALACHI

Superscription (1:1)

Malachi 1:1

¹An oracle, the word of Yahweh to Israel by the hand of Malachi.

מַשָּׂא דְבַר־יְהוָה אֶל־יִשְׂרָאֵל בְּיַד מַלְאָכִי: 1:1

The opening, nonverbal sentence is a narrative discourse of classification for the book and serves as a title. The sentence begins with a noun, which classifies the entire book as oracular in nature and sets the stage for the remainder of the book. The narrative identifies the giver and recipient of the oracles as well as the mediator between the two.

מַשָּׂא דְבַר־יְהוָה. Zech 9:1 and 12:1 also use this phrase with similar grammatical construction as found here.

מַשָּׂא. Noun m s, perhaps constr (Niccacci, 70) but probably in apposition, such as in the many uses of מַשָּׂא in Isaiah's prophecies against the nations (chs. 13–23), with the remainder of the verse defining the nature of this oracle. The word מַשָּׂא indicates the nature of the book. The word can be translated "oracle" (as in Isa 13:1; 15:1; 17:1; Jer 23:33) or "burden" (as in Isa 22:25; see BDB, 672). Both meanings are theologically appropriate in the context of Malachi. (See Stuart, 1277–78, for a lengthy discussion on מַשָּׂא).

דְבַר־יְהוָה. Noun m s constr – pr noun, the tetragrammaton for Yahweh. This construct genitival phrase designates the source and authority of the oracle.

אֶל־יִשְׂרָאֵל. Prep – pr noun. Prepositional phrase identifying the oracle's recipients. The preposition אֶל marks a dative (WO §11.2.2a) and identifies the object of דְּבַר־יְהוָה.

בְּיַד מַלְאָכִי. Prep בְּ with noun f s constr + noun m s constr with 1 c s pronominal suf. Genitival phrase indicating the deliverer of the oracle. The circumstantial usage of the בְּ preposition is a genitive of authorship, denoting the writer or speaker (WO §9.5.1c). Hill indicates that the preposition demonstrates a human agent speaking for the divine and should be translated "though" (Hill, 134). The noun is either a title with a first common singular pronominal suffix or a proper name. The LXX has the phrase ἀγγέλλου αὐτοῦ "his angel" using the third person pronoun instead of first person (*BHS* note 1ᵃ). The Targum of Jonathan adds "who is called the scribe Ezra" associating the person with Ezra (Watts, 375). Many scholars think מַלְאָכִי refers to a title rather than a personal name. Tate connects "my messenger" to the "messenger" named in 3:1 and says that the term refers to a function of the priests, as described in 2:7 (Tate, 391).

First Oracle: God Loves Jacob (1:2-5)

Malachi 1:2-5

²"I love you," says Yahweh. But you say, "In what way do you love us? Is not Esau a brother to Jacob?" The declaration of Yahweh. "And I loved Jacob; ³but I hated Esau and I made his mountain a desolation and his inheritance for jackals of a wilderness. ⁴Though Edom says, 'we have been beaten down, but we again will rebuild the ruins.'" Thus says Yahweh of hosts, "They may build but I will tear down. And they shall call them a territory of wickedness, and the people with whom Yahweh is indignant forever. ⁵And your eyes will see and you, you will say, 'Yahweh is great above the territory of Israel.'"

The first oracle takes the form of prophetic disputation. Here, the author employs the catechetical or question and answer style using pseudo-dialogue. This oracle begins with one of a series of rhetorical questions and answers presented in the first person from Yahweh. The three-part structure is as follows: the prophet (or Yahweh) makes a statement of fact, the audience disputes the statement by voicing objections with a question, and the prophet restates the fact supported with evidence (Smith, 304), or as Hill says declaration, refutation, and rebuttal (Hill, 259). The writer uses these questions to condemn his audience. Also, the writer uses antithetical word pairs (such as יַעֲקֹב and עֵשָׂו) throughout this section to heighten the disparity between the people and Yahweh (see GM, 31). This section contains chiasms, such as in verse 2:

A "I love,"

   B "says Yahweh,"

B´ "you say,"

A´ "you love."

Also, this section has parallelism. Verse 3 has synonymous parallelism:

"I made his mountain a desolation

and his inheritance for jackals of a wilderness."

The word pairs in this section demonstrate antithetical parallelism, as in verse 2b-3a:

"I loved Jacob,

but I hated Esau."

In this case, both the verb and objects are antithetically paralleled.

Key Words				
אָהַב	אֱדוֹם	בָּנָה	הָרַס	יַעֲקֹב
יִשְׂרָאֵל	עֵשָׂו	רְשָׁעָה	שָׂנֵא	

1:2   אָהַבְתִּי אֶתְכֶם אָמַר יְהוָה וַאֲמַרְתֶּם בַּמֶּה אֲהַבְתָּנוּ
הֲלוֹא־אָח עֵשָׂו לְיַעֲקֹב נְאֻם־יְהוָה וָאֹהַב אֶת־יַעֲקֹב:

Verse 2 begins the first oracle which is written in oracular prose in the form of a prophetic dispute with a statement from Yahweh.

אָהַבְתִּי אֶתְכֶם. Qal *qatal* 1 c s √אָהַב + sign of dir obj with 2 m pl pronominal suf. The *qatal* verb indicates an action completed in past time but extending into the present that can be translated into English in the present tense (GKC §106*g*; Stuart, 1281). This phrase is dialogue and is the opening statement Yahweh uses for Yahweh's arguments against the people. It also serves as the general theme of the book. אָהַב is a word associated with and foundational of the covenant in Deuteronomy. Els suggests that אָהַב expresses an "act of election in sovereign grace" while keeping the idea of a feeling of affection (*NIDOT*, 1:282).

אָמַר יְהֹוָה. Qal *qatal* 3 m s √אָמַר + pr noun. Discourse in past time identifying Yahweh as the speaker. This is an abbreviated messenger formula and is a common phrase found in Amos, Haggai, Zechariah, and Malachi marking divine speeches. See note in 1:4 and 3:13 below.

וַאֲמַרְתֶּם. Qal *weqatal* 2 m pl √אָמַר. The *waw* indicates a continuation of the narrative in past time and serves as an adversative conjunction, translated as "but" in English, indicating a reversal of thought. In this case, Yahweh echoes the objection of the people. The second use of אָמַר indicates a desire for understanding (Hill, 147).

בַּמָּה אֲהַבְתָּנוּ. בְּ prep with interrog pron + Qal *qatal* 1 c pl √אָהַב. Discourse using the same Hebrew root words as Yahweh's opening statement, indicating grammatical continuity but theological division, that is, the phrase is opposed to what Yahweh says. בַּמָּה is a combination of the בְּ preposition and the interrogative מָה, and is translated "in what" or "how." This form occurs only here and in 2:17 in Malachi while בַּמֶּה is used in 1:6, 7; 3:7, 8.

הֲלוֹא־אָח עֵשָׂו לְיַעֲקֹב. Interrog הֲ with neg adv – noun m s + pr noun + לְ prep with pr noun. Interrogative statement of comparison. The interrogative הֲ and the negative adverb form a double negative that anticipates an affirmative assent rather than a vocal answer (Hill, 148). עֵשָׂו לְיַעֲקֹב are in diametrical apposition, both to the two brothers in Genesis, Jacob and Esau, and to Judah and Edom. Both are illustrative of the diametrical apposition between Yahweh's and Israel's אָהַב. Note that in the post-exilic period only Judah remained of what was the country Israel under the United Monarchy. The term "Israel" is a common term post-exilic writers used for an idealized state, but refers to the remnant, which is Judah. The לְ preposition on לְיַעֲקֹב begins a periphrastic genitive construction and indicates possession (Hill, 150).

נְאָם־יְהֹוָה. Noun m s constr – pr noun. Abbreviated messenger formula. This is a common phrase, a nominal exclamation (Hill, 150), used in the middle of and at the end of divine oracles to indicate an interruption of or closure of thought and adding divine authority (cf Jer 23:23). This phrase separates the prior argument and the restatement and expounding of Yahweh's thesis that follows. *BHS* critical apparatus note 2[a-a] suggests deleting the phrase because it interrupts the metrical flow of the text (*BHS*, 1081), however, this omission would detract from the authoritative nature this phrase gives to the text.

וָאֹהַב אֶת־יַעֲקֹב. Qal *wayyiqtol* 1 c s √אָהֵב + sign of dir obj – pr noun. The sentence is the beginning of a comparative discourse that continues in verse 3. The *waw* relative indicates consequence and can be translated "yet." This phrase affirms the thesis statement found in the first part of this verse. The *wayyiqtol* form of אָהֵב perhaps functions in a double role of completed and progressive state of Yahweh's relationship with his people—he has loved and continues to love (see WO §22.2.3b). This phrase and the first phrase of verse 3 form a grammatical chiastic structure: verb/object//object/verb.

וְאֶת־עֵשָׂו שָׂנֵאתִי וָאָשִׂים אֶת־הָרָיו שְׁמָמָה וְאֶת־   1:3   נַחֲלָתוֹ לְתַנּוֹת מִדְבָּר׃

וְאֶת־עֵשָׂו שָׂנֵאתִי. *Waw* advers + sign of dir obj – pr noun + Qal *qatal* 1 c s √שָׂנֵא. The object עֵשָׂו is placed first to complete the chiastic structure with יַעֲקֹב began in the last phrase of verse 2.

וְאֶת־עֵשָׂו. *Waw* advers (see AC, 294). The rivaling twins of Genesis, Esau and Jacob, are parallel in thought to Edom and Judah. This parallelism is obvious in the last part of this verse.

שָׂנֵאתִי. This word is a strong stative verb functioning in stark contrast (an antithesis) to אָהֵב, just as עֵשָׂו contrasts יַעֲקֹב (see KD, 637). שָׂנֵא and אָהֵב are polar opposites, often antithetically paralleled, as they are here. This verbal word pair is commonly used in prophetic literature to express opposite emotions or opposite positions in Yahweh's covenant relationship (e.g., see Amos 5:15). In this context, שָׂנֵא has more of the sense of not chosen rather the emotion of malcontent (*NIDOT*, 3:1257).

וָאָשִׂים אֶת־הָרָיו שְׁמָמָה וְאֶת־נַחֲלָתוֹ לְתַנּוֹת מִדְבָּר. This narrative phrase expounds on the previous phrase and uses a *wayyiqtol* verb to govern two synonymously paralleled objects.

וָאָשִׂים. Qal *wayyiqtol* 1 c s √שִׂים. Continuation and expansion of the narrative based upon the past time state of שָׂנֵאתִי as indicated by the *waw* consecutive.

אֶת־הָרָיו שְׁמָמָה וְאֶת־נַחֲלָתוֹ לְתַנּוֹת מִדְבָּר. The signs of the direct object identify parallel objects. They are matched with third masculine singular pronominal suffixes on construct nouns.

אֶת־הָרָיו שְׁמָמָה. Sign of dir obj – noun m pl constr with 3 m s pronominal suf + noun f s. This pronouncement against Edom is similar to the one in Joel 4:19 (Hill, 154).

וְאֶת־נַחֲלָתוֹ לְתַנּוֹת מִדְבָּר. *Waw* cop + sign of dir obj – noun f s constr with 3 m s pronominal suf + לְ prep + noun f pl constr + noun m s. לְתַנּוֹת מִדְבָּר may be understood as the indirect object of both הָרָיו שְׁמָמָה and נַחֲלָתוֹ (see Hill, 154). The לְ preposition indicates an indirect object of a goal (WO §11.2.10d). The LXX has an alternate reading to this phrase. Instead of "jackals of a wilderness," the LXX has εἰς δώματα ἐρήμου meaning "dwellings in a wilderness." The Vulgate has *dracones*, meaning "serpents of a wilderness" (Hill, 155). However, the Masoretic Text reading makes sense and should be retained.

נַחֲלָתוֹ is covenant language, presented here as reflecting negatively upon Edom.

1:4   כִּי־תֹאמַר אֱדוֹם רֻשַּׁשְׁנוּ וְנָשׁוּב וְנִבְנֶה חֳרָבוֹת כֹּה
אָמַר יְהוָה צְבָאוֹת הֵמָּה יִבְנוּ וַאֲנִי אֶהֱרוֹס וְקָרְאוּ
לָהֶם גְּבוּל רִשְׁעָה וְהָעָם אֲשֶׁר־זָעַם יְהוָה עַד־עוֹלָם:

Verse 4 is a contrast between Edom and God's intentions, continuing the theme of verse 3.

כִּי־תֹאמַר אֱדוֹם רֻשַּׁשְׁנוּ וְנָשׁוּב וְנִבְנֶה חֳרָבוֹת. Conditional clause of situation (Hill, 156).

כִּי. Adverb of condition functioning as a causal conjunction with a sense of "though" or "because" (AC, 149).

תֹאמַר. Qal *yiqtol* 3 f s √אָמַר. This form could be second masculine singular.

אֱדוֹם. Pr noun f. Subject of the clause. Although normally masculine, אֱדוֹם is feminine here, as in Jer 49:17 and Ezek 32:29. For a discussion on why the feminine form is used here, see KD, 638.

רֻשַּׁשְׁנוּ. Pu *qatal* 1 c pl √רָשַׁשׁ. רֻשַּׁשְׁנוּ is a verb of condition with completed action in past time. This verb is used only here and in Jer 5:17 and is used in conjunction with the destruction of cities (BDB, 958).

וְנָשׁוּב וְנִבְנֶה. Qal *wᵉyiqtol* 1 c pl √שׁוּב + Qal *wᵉyiqtol* 1 c pl √בָּנָה. The phrase begins with an adversative conjunction indicating a change in discourse direction and tense. It has a disjunctive function and is translated "but." וְנָשׁוּב is an auxiliary and functioning adverbially, translated "but again" (WO §39.3.1b). See a similar construction with וְשַׁבְתֶּם וּרְאִיתֶם in 3:18 below. The *wᵉyiqtol* form of בָּנָה has force of purpose and indicates future intention.

חֳרָבוֹת. Noun f pl. Dir obj of וְנִבְנֶה. Noun commonly used as a consequence in judgment oracles in Jeremiah and Ezekiel but used only here in Malachi.

כֹּה אָמַר יְהוָה צְבָאוֹת הֵמָּה יִבְנוּ וַאֲנִי אֶהֱרוֹס. Consequence clause introduced with the forceful particle כֹּה.

כֹּה אָמַר יְהוָה צְבָאוֹת. Demons adv + Qal *qatal* 3 m s √אָמַר + pr noun + noun m pl. This is an expanded messenger formula common to prophetic literature. The formula, without כֹּה, is common in Malachi. However, this occurrence is the only one in Malachi where the phrase is prefaced with כֹּה at the beginning of the verse. כֹּה marks a reversal of action, which began with כִּי. Hill points out that this phrase is a "customary formal opening to a divine oracle"

(Hill, 157). The use of יְהוָה צְבָאוֹת is common in Isaiah, Jeremiah, Haggai, and Zechariah. The writer uses the messenger formula 24 times in 54 verses (see chart 2 in the Appendix for list of occurrences of the messenger formula in Malachi). Hill says the prophet's high frequency of the messenger formula's usage "certainly emphasizes the divine origin of his message and connects his oracles with earlier prophetic traditions" (Hill, 158). Furthermore, Hill says this suggests a crisis of authority in post-exilic Judah (Hill, 158). For more information on the messenger formula, see Westermann, 98ff.

הֵמָּה יִבְנוּ וַאֲנִי אֶהֱרוֹס. Indep pers pron 3 m pl + Qal *yiqtol* 3 m pl jus √בָּנָה + *waw* advers with indep pers pron 1 c s + Qal *yiqtol* 1 c s √הָרַס. Personal pronouns, the subjects of the verbs, have been intentionally added and placed first for emphasis. The phrase demonstrates the antithesis between Edom and Yahweh. The use of the jussive mood of יִבְנוּ emphasizes the inferior abilities of Edom "to build" against the more emphatic אֶהֱרוֹס stressing the superior abilities of Yahweh "to tear down" (Hill, 158). הָרַס means to "tear down" as in the destruction of a building; however, when the verb is used with Yahweh as the subject, it also has the connotation of judgment (*NIDOT*, 1:1061).

וְקָרְאוּ לָהֶם גְּבוּל רִשְׁעָה וְהָעָם אֲשֶׁר־זָעַם יְהוָה עַד־עוֹלָם׃. Pejorative clause of consequence with an unidentified third common plural subject.

וְקָרְאוּ לָהֶם. Qal *wᵉqatal* 3 c pl √קָרָא + לְ prep with 3 m pl pronominal suf. The *waw* conjunction is consequential, having the sense of "then" (see AC, 147–48). לָהֶם is the indirect object of קָרְאוּ. The לְ preposition marks the goal of an action (WO §11.2.10d; cf. GKC §119*t*).

גְּבוּל רִשְׁעָה. Noun m s constr + noun f s. This genitival construct phrase functions as a derogatory epithet (Hill, 159) and is the direct object of וְקָרְאוּ. רִשְׁעָה is also found in Mal 3:15.

וְהָעָם אֲשֶׁר־זָעַם יְהוָה עַד־עוֹלָם. *Waw* cop with def art and noun m s + rel pron – Qal *qatal* 3 m s √זָעַם + pr noun + prep – noun m s. Second dir obj of the clause. The relative pronoun introduces a stative verbal phrase in normal verb/subject order.

זָעַם. The Qal *qatal* verb of completed action adds emphasis to Yahweh's resolve and emotion. It functions here to show the result of Yahweh's judgment.

יְהוָה. Subj of זָעַם.

עַד־עוֹלָם. Prepositional phrase indicating long temporal duration. עוֹלָם also occurs in Mal 3:4. עַד־עוֹלָם does not mean "forever" but rather long duration (Stuart, 1289–90).

1:5   וְעֵינֵיכֶם תִּרְאֶינָה וְאַתֶּם תֹּאמְרוּ יִגְדַּל יְהוָה מֵעַל
לִגְבוּל יִשְׂרָאֵל:

Verse 5 is the end of the first oracle. This oracle ends as it began, with a statement from Yahweh but in future time here rather than in past time as in verse 2.

וְעֵינֵיכֶם תִּרְאֶינָה. *Waw* cop with noun f pl constr and 2 m pl pronominal suf + Qal *yiqtol* 3 f pl √רָאָה. The position of the noun first places emphasis on the subject and makes the statement more personal to the recipient. The *waw* + a nonverb indicate a disjunction, signaling a shift in a scene or change in action (WO §39.2.3a). In this case, it indicates the end of the oracle. The *yiqtol* form here indicates future time.

וְאַתֶּם תֹּאמְרוּ. *Waw* cop with indep pers pron 2 m pl + Qal *yiqtol* 2 m pl √אָמַר. This phrase has parallel construction with the preceding phrase, emphasizing the subject. Hill suggests this construction represents a heightening of emotion (Hill, 160).

יִגְדַּל יְהוָה מֵעַל לִגְבוּל יִשְׂרָאֵל. Discourse in verb/subj/obj order. This statement closes the oracle and indicates a settlement of the dispute.

יִגְדַּל. Qal *yiqtol* 3 m s √גָּדַל. The *yiqtol* form here implies a current and continuing state. The *yiqtol* form could be jussive form here, thus softening up the phrase to "Let Yahweh be great. . . ."

יְהֹוָה. Subj of יִגְדַּל.

מֵעַל לִגְבוּל יִשְׂרָאֵל. Prep + לְ prep with noun m s constr + pr noun. The word מֵעַל contains two prepositions, a blending of עַל and מִן. This combination has the sense of "higher than" or "upwards" (BDB, 751) or "above" (KD, 638). Stuart argues for the more figurative sense of "beyond" (Stuart, 1292). The use of גְּבוּל is reminiscent of and in diametrical apposition to its use in verse 4. The לְ preposition is superfluous in this phrase. *BHS* critical apparatus note 5ᵃ suggests that it is dittography from the final לְ of the previous word.

Second Oracle: Sinful Priests (1:6–2:9)

The second oracle is the longest of the oracles in Malachi; therefore, I have separated it into four subunits: 1:6-8, 9-13, 14; and 2:1-9. This oracle continues in prophetic disputation discourse, much like the first oracle, using a pseudo-dialogue of questions and answers at first (1:6-14) and then followed by prophetic diatribe (2:1-9) that expands on concepts introduced in the questions and answers. The writer employs irony, sarcasm, and satire, as well as synonymous parallelism, but does not use word pairs as in the first oracle. This oracle differs from the previous one in that the writer focuses on the priests rather than the general population of Israel. The speaker of the second oracle is Yahweh and is presented in first person speech.

Key Words				
אָרַר	בָּזָה	בְּרִית	בְּרָכָה	יָרֵא
נָגַשׁ	כָּבֵד	שֵׁם	תּוֹרַת	

Malachi 1:6-8

⁶"A son honors a father and a servant his master. If I am a father, where is my honor, and if I am a master where is my respect?" says Yahweh of hosts to you, priests, despisers of my name. But you say, "How have we despised your name?" ⁷"Offering upon my altar defiled food." But you say, "How have we defiled you?" When you say, "The table of Yahweh, it is despised. ⁸And when you present a blind [animal] to sacrifice, there is no evil! And when you present a lame and sick [animal], there is no evil!

Bring it near to your governor! Will he be pleased with you, or will he lift up your face?" says Yahweh of hosts.

1:6   בֵּ֣ן יְכַבֵּ֣ד אָ֔ב וְעֶ֖בֶד אֲדֹנָ֑יו וְאִם־אָ֣ב אָ֗נִי אַיֵּ֤ה כְבוֹדִי֙ וְאִם־אֲדוֹנִ֣ים אָ֗נִי אַיֵּ֤ה מוֹרָאִי֙ אָמַ֣ר | יְהוָ֣ה צְבָא֗וֹת לָכֶם֙ הַכֹּֽהֲנִים֙ בּוֹזֵ֣י שְׁמִ֔י וַאֲמַרְתֶּ֕ם בַּמֶּ֥ה בָזִ֖ינוּ אֶת־ שְׁמֶֽךָ:

בֵּ֣ן יְכַבֵּ֣ד אָ֔ב וְעֶ֖בֶד אֲדֹנָ֑יו. Noun m s + Pi *yiqtol* 3 m s √ כָּבַד + noun m s + *waw* cop with noun m s + noun m s constr with 3 m s pronominal suf. This phrase is an anacoenosis; an appeal to others based upon common interest (Hill, 174). This phrase contains two generic expressions in apposition. These are proverbs, sayings that were commonly held to be true.

בֵּ֣ן. Subj of יְכַבֵּ֣ד.

יְכַבֵּ֣ד. Piel *yiqtol* form is not jussive and implies a timeless sense of ongoing action, which Waltke and O'Connor call progressive nonperfective (WO §31.3b). כָּבַד has the meaning of "be heavy" but also means "honor." Collins says proper "honor" is in one's response to God's saving activity, usually in some form of worship (*NIDOT*, 2:579).

אָב. Obj of יְכַבֵּ֣ד.

וְעֶ֖בֶד אֲדֹנָ֑יו. Verbless construct noun phrase in apposition to בֵּ֣ן יְכַבֵּ֣ד אָב expressing relationship with its implied verbal meaning derived from יְכַבֵּ֣ד. The missing verb of a second, parallel clause is a common poetic feature in the Hebrew Bible, often referred to as "gapping." אֲדֹנָ֑יו means "his lord" or "his master," referring to a suzerain (Hill, 174).

וְאִם־אָ֣ב אָ֗נִי אַיֵּ֤ה כְבוֹדִי֙. A verbless clause of identification (Hill, 175).

וְאִם־אָ֣ב. *Waw* conj with hypothetical part – noun m s. The *waw*

is conjunctive and connects these clauses with the prior section. אִם
is a hypothetical particle and makes the clause conditional, translated
as "if" in English.

אַיֵּה כְבוֹדִי. Interrog + noun m s constr with 1 c s pronominal suf.
The main clause is an interrogative response to the preceding conditional clause. The apodosis usually starts with a *waw* meaning "then"
in English but it missing here. כְבוֹדִי is the nominal form of כָּבַד and
carries the same meaning as above and in 2:2.

וְאִם־אֲדוֹנִים אָנִי אַיֵּה מוֹרָאִי. Second verbless conditional
clause with an interrogative main clause. The construction is the same
as the previous one.

וְאִם־אֲדוֹנִים. *Waw* conj with part – noun m pl abs. Plural noun
with a singular meaning. Smith suggests this is a plural of majesty
(Smith, 309, note 6b).

מוֹרָאִי. Noun m s constr with 1c s pronominal suf. The writer uses
this word in the second proverb but it is not used in the first proverb
at the beginning of this verse. The word also occurs in 2:5. The LXX
adds φοβηθήσεται, the Greek verb for "fear," to the proverb to complete the parallelism here (Smith, 309). מוֹרָאִי is the nominal form of
יָרֵא meaning "fear." מוֹרָא, appearing twelve times in the Masoretic
Text, often carries the connotation of worship. Here, it has the sense
of "respect" for one in a position higher than oneself (*NIDOT*, 2:532).

אָמַר | יְהוָה צְבָאוֹת לָכֶם. Qal *qatal* 3 m s + pr noun + noun
m pl abs + לְ prep with 2 m p pronominal suf. This is a common, prophetic messenger formula and is repeated eleven times in the second
oracle: 1:6, 8, 9, 10, 11, 13 [2x], 14; 2:2, 4, and 8); however, this is the
only occurrence with לָכֶם.

לָכֶם. The dative לְ preposition marks the indirect object of אָמַר
(WO §11.2.10d).

הַכֹּהֲנִים בּוֹזֵי שְׁמִי. Dir obj of Yahweh's speech. The phrase has
a vocative sense.

בּוֹזֵי שְׁמִי. Qal act ptc m pl constr √בָּזָה + noun m s constr with

1 c s pronominal suf. This participial phrase functions adjectivally and is descriptive of the noun הַכֹּהֲנִים. The participial form suggests continuous action. בָּזָה occurs 43 times in the Masoretic Text and has the meaning of "despise" as in undervaluing a person's worth or attributing little value. Grisanti says that "*bzh* denotes an inner attitude, it clearly impacts relationships" (*NIDOT*, 1:628). בָּזָה is an antonym of כָּבַד and functions as such here. The noun שֵׁם is a major element in the second oracle and occurs eight times (1:6 [2x], 11 [3x], 14; 2:2, 5). The noun is a synonym for God's name Yahweh. Ross says שֵׁם can have the connotation of "reputation," which is the case here (*NIDOT*, 4:148).

וַאֲמַרְתֶּם בַּמֶּה בָזִינוּ אֶת־שְׁמֶךָ: Discourse with an interrogative clause.

וַאֲמַרְתֶּם. *Waw* advers with Qal *qatal* 2 m pl √אָמַר. וַאֲמַרְתֶּם introduces the priest's objection, as told by Yahweh.

בַּמֶּה בָזִינוּ אֶת־שְׁמֶךָ. בְּ prep with interrog part + Qal *qatal* 1 c p √בָּזַה + sign of dir obj + noun m s constr with 2 m s pronominal suf. This clause of objection continues the discourse; however, the writer uses בַּמֶּה instead of אַיֵּה. The בַּמֶּה combination of preposition and interrogative literally means of "wherein" (BDB, 553) but it is an inquiry of the manner in which something is done, thus it is best translated "how" in this case. בָּזָה connotes "disloyalty" or "breach of covenant" when used in a context discussing covenant (Hill, 176). See note on בָּזָה above.

1:7   מַגִּישִׁים עַל־מִזְבְּחִי לֶחֶם מְגֹאָל וַאֲמַרְתֶּם בַּמֶּה גֵאַלְנוּךָ בֶּאֱמָרְכֶם שֻׁלְחַן יְהוָה נִבְזֶה הוּא:

מַגִּישִׁים עַל־מִזְבְּחִי לֶחֶם מְגֹאָל. Instead of citing proverbs as in verse 6, the writer uses direct accusation against the priests.

מַגִּישִׁים. Hiph ptc m pl abs √נָגַשׁ. The clause lacks a subject but assumes the pronoun "you." Since the clause is disjunctive from the previous clause (based on context), a subject has to be supplied (see GKC §116s). It answers the question of the previous clause. נָגַשׁ means to "bring near" but in the Hiphil has the meaning of "offer."

עַל־מִזְבְּחִי. Prep – n m s constr with 1 c s pronominal suf. Indir obj of מַגִּישִׁים. The עַל preposition has a locational sense (WO §11.2.13b).

לֶחֶם מְגֹאָל. Noun m s + Pu ptc m s abs √גָּאַל. Dir obj of מַגִּישִׁים. מְגֹאָל is participle functioning as an adjective describing לֶחֶם. Here, the writer may be using the secondary meaning of גָּאַל, which is "defile" rather than its primary meaning of "redeem" (BDB, 145–46). However, Averbeck suggests גָּאַל is a byform of גָּעַל which means "defiled" (NIDOT, 1:794; see TDOT, 3:46). לֶחֶם literally means "bread" but the word is referring to animal sacrifices here (Hill, 177–78; Verhoef, 216–17; cf Hag 2:12).

וַאֲמַרְתֶּם בַּמֶּה גֵאַלְנוּךָ. Discourse with interrogative clause.

וַאֲמַרְתֶּם. Waw advers with Qal qatal 2 m pl √אָמַר. This phrase is identical to the one in verse 6 and introduces the priest's objection, as told by Yahweh.

בַּמֶּה גֵאַלְנוּךָ. ב prep with interrog + Pi qatal 1 c pl √גָּאַל with 2 m s pronominal suf. Interrogative phrase carries the force of an objection, with the preposition and interrogative combination בַּמֶּה being translated "how," as in the previous interrogative discourse.

בֶּאֱמָרְכֶם שֻׁלְחַן יְהוָה נִבְזֶה הוּא: Discourse answering the previous interrogative.

בֶּאֱמָרְכֶם. ב prep with Qal inf constr √אָמַר and 2 m pl pronominal suf. The preposition ב is used in a temporal sense taking on the meaning of "when" (WO §36.2.2b). When a pronominal suffix is used with an infinitive in this construction, it functions as the subject while the infinitive acts like a finite verb (WO §36.6.2b).

שֻׁלְחַן יְהוָה. Noun m s constr + pr noun. Subj of the clause. שֻׁלְחַן does not mean table, as in the Table for the Bread of Presence (Exod 25:30), but is synonymously paralleled to מִזְבֵּח (Hill, 178).

The phrase is unique to Malachi in the Hebrew Bible, used here and in 1:12.

נִבְזֶה הוּא. Niph ptc m s abs √בָּזָה + indep pers pron 3 m s. Participial clause of identification. See note on בָּזָה in 1:6. The Niphal participle has a passive meaning with a sense of the state of being of the subject and functions here with the force of an adjective (KD, 640). The prophet uses the Niphal participle form (נִבְזֶה) three times in his dispute discourses: 1:7, 12; 2:9. The personal pronoun functions as the subject and is superfluous in this clause. However, the pronoun may be a pleonastic pronoun, simply a redundant word (WO §8.4.1b).

1:8 וְכִי־תַגִּשׁוּן עִוֵּר לִזְבֹּחַ אֵין רָע וְכִי תַגִּישׁוּ פִּסֵּחַ וְחֹלֶה
אֵין רָע הַקְרִיבֵהוּ נָא לְפֶחָתֶךָ הֲיִרְצְךָ אוֹ הֲיִשָּׂא פָנֶיךָ
אָמַר יְהוָה צְבָאוֹת׃

Verse 8 begins a series of ironic statements and questions that are not meant to be taken literally. They demand a negative response.

וְכִי־תַגִּשׁוּן עִוֵּר לִזְבֹּחַ אֵין רָע. The first sarcastic statement of this series.

וְכִי־תַגִּשׁוּן. *Waw* cop with conj – Hiph *yiqtol* 2 m p √נָגַשׁ. The *waw* copulative connects this clause with the previous one. The כִּי conjunction takes on a temporal sense "when," continuing this nuance from the previous verse. תַגִּשׁוּן parallels the same word's usage in verse 7, further bonding their interconnectedness. Waltke and O'Connor say the final *nun* in תַגִּשׁוּן is a *nun paragogicum* and indicates contrast (WO §31.7.1a). In this case, the contrast indicates that the priests' actions are opposite to what is expected.

עִוֵּר לִזְבֹּחַ. Noun m s + לְ prep with Qal inf constr √זָבַח. The noun functions as the direct object of תַגִּשׁוּן while the לְ preposition marks the infinitive as the indirect object (Hill, 179).

אֵין רָע. Neg subst constr + noun m s. אֵין functions as a particle of negation in this verbless clause (BDB, 34). The phrase is ambiguous.

Some scholars translate the clause as a question (Smith, 307) while others treat it as an ironic statement (Hill, 180; KD, 640). The lack of an interrogative, which is present in previous interrogative clauses, and Malachi's use of irony in previous verses suggest that the correct translation is as an ironic statement.

וְכִי תַגִּישׁוּ פִּסֵּחַ וְחֹלֶה אֵין רָע. This clause is paralleled synonymously to the previous clause, differentiated only by the direct object.

תַגִּישׁוּ. Hiph *yiqtol* 2 m p √נָגַשׁ. See comments on this verb in the phrase above.

פִּסֵּחַ וְחֹלֶה. Noun m s + *waw* cop with Qal act ptc m s abs √חָלָה. Dir obj of תַגִּישׁוּ. The participle חֹלֶה functions substantively as a noun.

הַקְרִיבֵהוּ נָא לְפֶחָתֶךָ. A command.

הַקְרִיבֵהוּ נָא. Hiph impv 2 m s √קָרַב with 3 m s pronominal suf + part of entreaty. The Hiphil form of קָרַב means "bring near" or "offer" and is used sarcastically here. The pronominal suffix is the direct object. The particle נָא usually makes the imperative more emphatic or urgent. (See the discussion on נָא in WO §34.7; Kelley, 173.) Lambdin calls it a modal particle that shows the command is a consequence of the previous statement (Lambdin, 170). Waltke and O'Connor and Lambdin argue that the particle should not be translated.

לְפֶחָתֶךָ. לְ prep with noun m s constr and 2 m s pronominal suf. Indir obj of the clause. The לְ preposition is dative of a goal or objective. The noun is unusual in Hebrew and generally refers to non-Israelite leaders. The noun פֶחָת is juxtaposed to יְהוָה in verse 7, distinguishing between the realms of "your governor" and "my altar" (Hill, 181).

הֲיִרְצְךָ אוֹ הֲיִשָּׂא פָנֶיךָ אָמַר יְהוָה צְבָאוֹת: The two interrogative clauses beginning with interrogative particles grammatically are simple questions. Gesenius points out that this construction can indicate a rhetorical question with an implied answer of "no," as the case is here (GKC §150*d*).

הֲיִרְצָֽךְ. Interrog ה with Qal *yiqtol* 3m s √רָצָה and 2 m s pronominal suf. Malachi uses the Qal *yiqtol* verb in its common future sense.
A *yiqtol* form of רָצָה appears in 1:8, 10, and 13 and has the idea of
acceptance of a gift or sacrifice (Hill, 181).

אוֹ הֲיִשָּׂא פָנֶיךָ. Conj + interrog ה with Qal *yiqtol* 3 m s √נָשָׂא +
noun m pl constr with 2 m s pronominal suf. אוֹ functions as a coordinating conjunction separating two clauses in the main clause that
present alternatives (WO §39.2.6b). This conjunction is used only
here and in 2:17 in Malachi. The noun phrase is an idiom for a happy
or favorable countenance. Hill suggests translating this phrase as an
idiom, "accepting someone kindly, be favorably disposed toward"
(Hill, 181).

אָמַר יְהוָה צְבָאוֹת. This prophetic messenger formula concludes and adds authority to verses 6-8. See discussion of the messenger formula in 1:4.

Malachi 1:9-13

[9]*"And now entreat the face of God, so that he will show us favor! From
your hand was this. Will he lift up your faces?," says Yahweh of hosts.*
[10]*"Oh, that one among you shut the doors, so that you would not kindle
a fire under my altar for nothing. There is no pleasure in me with you,"
says the Yahweh of hosts, "and I will not accept an offering from your
hand.* [11]*For from the rising of the sun even to its setting my name is great
among the nations. In every place a burnt offering will be offered in my
name, and a clean offering, for my name is great among the nations," says
the Yahweh of hosts.* [12]*"But you are profaning it, when you say the table
of the Lord is defiled, and its fruit—contemptible is its food.* [13]*And you
say, 'Behold, what a weariness.' And you blow at it," says the Yahweh of
hosts. "And you bring torn and the lame and the sick and you bring for the
offering. Should I accept it from your hand?" says Yahweh.*

This section continues the oracular prophetic discourse with God
speaking for the priests in a sarcastic or ironic manner. In this section, God expounds upon the answers of verses 6-8. This section has

common vocabulary and structure with the previous one, intensifying their interconnectedness. It ends (verse 13) with an interrogative clause, reminiscent of the interrogatives of verses 6-8.

1:9 וְעַתָּה חַלּוּ־נָא פְנֵי־אֵל וִיחָנֵּנוּ מִיֶּדְכֶם הָיְתָה זֹּאת הֲיִשָּׂא מִכֶּם פָּנִים אָמַר יְהוָה צְבָאוֹת:

וְעַתָּה חַלּוּ־נָא פְנֵי־אֵל וִיחָנֵּנוּ. Discourse with God speaking for the priests.

וְעַתָּה. *Waw* cop with temp adv. The adverb serves as a discourse marker. The discourse turns from habitual past action to present and future action. The adverb separates the previous section from this one.

חַלּוּ־נָא. Pi impv 2 m pl √חָלָה – part of entreaty. חָלָה verb only occurs in the Piel so its meaning is not intensified by the Piel stem. The particle נָא, however, does intensify the command. See note on this particle in 1:8. The intensity of the particle adds to the irony (ridicule) of the statement (Verhoef, 220). The verb, meaning "entreat," is perhaps ironically paralleled to חֹלֶה "weak" in verse 8, in the sense of offering "weak ones" to Yahweh to make him "weak" (GM, 53).

פְנֵי־אֵל. Noun m pl constr – noun m s. Dir obj of חַלּוּ־נָא. The phrase is an idiom, meaning "entreat the favor of God" (Hill, 182).

וִיחָנֵּנוּ. Qal *wᵉyiqtol* 3 m s √חָנַן with 1 c pl pronominal suf. According to Waltke and O'Connor, the imperative + *waw* + prefix conjugation signifying purpose or result (WO §34.6a; Hill, 182). The *wᵉyiqtol* verb is cohortative in form. The *waw* connects a clause of result with the previous clause and should be translated "so that."

מִיֶּדְכֶם הָיְתָה זֹּאת. Circumstantial verbal clause (see GKC §156d). Smith interprets this clause as a question although no interrogative is present in Hebrew (Smith, 308).

מִיֶּדְכֶם. מִן prep with noun f s and 2 m s pronominal suf. Indir obj of וִיחָנֵּנוּ. The מִן prefix is used in a causal sense, placing blame in this case (Hill, 183; Verhoef, 220). The indirect object is fronted before the verb for emphasis.

הָיְתָה. Qal *qatal* 3 f s √הָיָה. The *qatal* verb is an indefinite perfect and has a sense of past, nonspecific time (Hill, 183).

זֹאת. Rel pron with a nominative function.

הֲיִשָּׂא מִכֶּם פָּנִים אָמַר יְהוָה צְבָאוֹת. The subject of the action changes from the priests to God.

הֲיִשָּׂא מִכֶּם פָּנִים. Interrog ה with Qal *yiqtol* 3 m s √נָשָׂא + מִן prep with 2 m pl pronominal suf + noun m pl. Interrogative clause. The clause is an idiom, reminiscent of a similar clause in 1:8.

אָמַר יְהוָה צְבָאוֹת. This prophetic messenger formula adds authority (see note in 1:4).

1:10 מִי גַם־בָּכֶם וְיִסְגֹּר דְּלָתַיִם וְלֹא־תָאִירוּ מִזְבְּחִי חִנָּם
אֵין־לִי חֵפֶץ בָּכֶם אָמַר יְהוָה צְבָאוֹת וּמִנְחָה לֹא־
אֶרְצֶה מִיֶּדְכֶם:

מִי גַם־בָּכֶם וְיִסְגֹּר דְּלָתַיִם וְלֹא־תָאִירוּ מִזְבְּחִי חִנָּם. Desiderative clause stating a wish (GKC §151*a*). The combination of מִי and the *yiqtol* verb express a wish rather than a question. This sense applies to the whole clause. The adverb גַם adds intensity to the wish (GM, 54–55).

מִי גַם־בָּכֶם. Interrog + adv – Introductory clause. This phrase functions as the subject of the verb יִסְגֹּר. גַם is an emphatic adverb and introduces an intensive clause (GKC §153). Waltke and O'Connor call the בְ preposition on בָּכֶם a בְ marking a partitive, meaning identifying one person among several (WO §11.2.5f).

וְיִסְגֹּר דְּלָתַיִם. Qal *w*ᵉ*yiqtol* 3 m s √סָגַר + noun m dual. Coordinating *waw* and a *yiqtol* verb is an unmarked connector with the previous clause, thus the two clauses are interpreted in the same sense, i.e., as a wish (WO §33.4b).

וְלֹא־תָאִ֫ירוּ מִזְבְּחִי חִנָּם. *Waw* cop with neg part – Hiph *yiqtol* 2 m p √אור + noun m s constr with 1 c s pronominal suf + adv. The coordinating *waw* conjunction with the *yiqtol* verb has a consequential sense and maintains the modal nonperfective of desire (Hill, 184).

מִזְבְּחִי חִנָּם. Dir obj of תָאִירוּ. חִנָּם modifies מִזְבְּחִי and describes the results of a course of action.

אֵין־לִי חֵפֶץ בָּכֶם אָמַר יְהוָה צְבָאוֹת. Independent, verbless clause.

אֵין־לִי חֵפֶץ בָּכֶם. Neg adv constr – לְ prep with 1 c s pronominal suf + noun m s + בְּ prep with 2 m pl pronominal suf. Verbless clause negated by אֵין. חֵפֶץ is a predicate adjective signifying emotion. בָּכֶם is a בְּ preposition of specification indicating the realm of the action (WO §11.2.5e).

אָמַר יְהוָה צְבָאוֹת. The messenger formula interrupts the thought thereby adding force to the clause. *BHS* note 10[a–a] suggests that the phrase is added; however, this type of interruption is common in the Hebrew Bible, especially in prophetic literature.

וּמִנְחָה לֹא־אֶרְצֶה מִיֶּדְכֶם: This clause completes the thought in the preceding clause.

וּמִנְחָה. *Waw* conj with noun f s. Dir obj of לֹא־אֶרְצֶה and fronted before the verb for emphasis. The *waw* functions either as a conjunctive "and," as coordinator of alternate force "neither," or as an emphatic "indeed" (Hill, 185).

לֹא־אֶרְצֶה. Neg part – Qal *yiqtol* 1 c s √רָצָה. The verb suggests anticipated future action.

מִיֶּדְכֶם. Prep מִן with noun f s constr and 2 m pl pronominal suf. Indir obj of לֹא־אֶרְצֶה.

1:11 כִּי מִמִּזְרַח־שֶׁמֶשׁ וְעַד־מְבוֹאוֹ גָּדוֹל שְׁמִי בַּגּוֹיִם
וּבְכָל־מָקוֹם מֻקְטָר מֻגָּשׁ לִשְׁמִי וּמִנְחָה טְהוֹרָה כִּי־
גָדוֹל שְׁמִי בַּגּוֹיִם אָמַר יְהוָה צְבָאוֹת:

A few scholars believe verses 11-14 are a later addition (see Merrill, 381; *BHS* note 11[a]); however, these verses make sense in their context and should be considered original. Many scholars note the difficulty of translating verse 11, particularly the Hophal participles (GM, 55–61). The verse contains an A/B/B′/A′ chiasm with A and A′ being parallel phrases of גָּדוֹל שְׁמִי בַּגּוֹיִם and B and B′ being the offerings. Another possibility is that גָּדוֹל שְׁמִי is a refrain rather than a chiasm (GM, 57). The verbs in verse 11 are usually translated in present tense; however, the future tense here fits with the context. Glazier-McDonald makes a strong argument for using the future tense based upon context (GM, 60–61).

כִּי מִמִּזְרַח־שֶׁמֶשׁ וְעַד־מְבוֹאוֹ. This clause is a cosmic analogy and indicates totality of space (Hill, 186).

כִּי. The disputation nature of the passage suggests that the particle may be functioning as an emphatic adverb, which would be translated "indeed" (WO §39.3.4). However, it may be functioning simply as a logical marker with a causal sense, in which case it should be translated "for" (Hill, 186; Verhoef, 223).

מִמִּזְרַח־שֶׁמֶשׁ וְעַד־מְבוֹאוֹ. Prep מִן with noun m s constr – noun m s + *waw* cop with adv – noun m s constr with 3 m s pronominal suf. The clause indicates totality of space by using extremes. This is called a merismus (Stuart, 1306).

גָּדוֹל שְׁמִי בַּגּוֹיִם. Adj m s + noun m s constr with 1 c s pronominal suf + בְּ prep with def art and noun m pl. This is a simple verbless clause with the predicative usage of the adjective (Kelley, 46; MNK, 233–34). The בְּ preposition has a spatial sense, meaning "among" (WO §11.2.5b).

וּבְכָל־מָקוֹם מֻקְטָר מֻגָּשׁ לִשְׁמִי וּמִנְחָה טְהוֹרָה. Independent, declarative clause.

וּבְכָל־מָקוֹם. *Waw* cop with בְּ prep and noun m s constr – noun m s. The בְּ preposition has a spatial sense, translated "among" (WO §11.2.5b). מָקוֹם is a generic word of location, made universal with the addition of בְּכָל.

מֻקְטָר. Scholars debate the identification of this word's form. BDB calls it a noun masculine singular meaning "incense," while pointing out that it is a *hapax legomenon* (BDB, 883; and Verhoef, 224–25). Glazier-McDonald identifies the word as a Hophal participle, with the meaning of "burnt offering." She argues that this interpretation is in line with the broader context (GM, 56–57). Since the context is about offerings of animal sacrifices and not incense, interpreting the word as a Hophal participle and translating it substantively as "burnt offering" makes more sense. Therefore, מֻקְטָר is a Hophal participle masculine singular, meaning "burnt offering," and functions as the subject of the clause.

מֻגָּשׁ לִשְׁמִי. Hoph ptc m pl √נָגַשׁ + לְ prep with noun m s constr and 1 c s pronominal suf. The Hophal participle is functioning as an intransitive passive verb, meaning "is being offered." The writer uses forms of נָגַשׁ six times in Malachi as a description of priestly ministry, i.e., offering sacrifices (Hill, 188). לִשְׁמִי has a datival לְ preposition, which marks the indirect object of מֻגָּשׁ.

וּמִנְחָה טְהוֹרָה. *Waw* cop with noun f s + adj f s. The adjective functions in the attributive sense and is modifying the noun.

כִּי־גָדוֹל שְׁמִי בַּגּוֹיִם אָמַר יְהוָה צְבָאוֹת: functions as a causal adverb and transitions to the closing clause of the discourse. This clause is a repeat of an identical clause found earlier in the verse and ends the chiasm.

אָמַר יְהוָה צְבָאוֹת: The messenger formula signals the completion of the clause and sets up a transition at the beginning of verse 12.

1:12 וְאַתֶּם מְחַלְּלִים אוֹתוֹ בֶּאֱמָרְכֶם שֻׁלְחַן אֲדֹנָי מְגֹאָל הוּא וְנִיבוֹ נִבְזֶה אָכְלוֹ:

The disjunctive *waw* signals a change in the participants from the nations to the priests (whom the writer refers to in second person). The verse begins the second paragraph (verses 12-14) of the discourse and resumes the argument against the priests.

וְאַתֶּם מְחַלְּלִים אוֹתוֹ. *Waw* adver with indep pers pron 2 m pl + Pi ptc m pl abs √חָלַל + sign of dir obj with 3 m s pronominal suf. The Piel participle emphasizes a durative circumstance, that is, an ongoing action (WO §37.6b). The direct object אוֹתוֹ refers to שְׁמִי in verse 11.

בֶּאֱמָרְכֶם שֻׁלְחַן אֲדֹנָי מְגֹאָל הוּא וְנִיבוֹ נִבְזֶה אָכְלוֹ׃. This is a difficult clause to translate and many scholars try to emend it. However, emendation is not necessary to make sense of the text. שֻׁלְחַן אֲדֹנָי מְגֹאָל הוּא is in intentional parallel with verse 7 (Stuart, 1307).

בֶּאֱמָרְכֶם. בְּ prep with Qal inf constr and 2 m pl pronominal suf. The בְּ preposition with an infinitive construct and a pronominal suffix form a temporal clause where the infinitive has a sense of action close in time to another event (WO §36.2.2b). The pronominal suffix functions as the subject of the clause.

שֻׁלְחַן אֲדֹנָי. Noun m s constr + pr noun. The use of אֲדֹנָי instead of יְהוָה may be to show Yahweh's lordship over the table. I treat אֲדֹנָי as a proper noun when used as an alternate word for Yahweh. Owens identifies אֲדֹנָי as a noun masculine plural with a first common singular suffix "my lord" (Owens, 933). Johnston says that the first common singular ending is used as an expression of courtesy (*NIDOT*, 1:259). Although technically correct, this word is not translated as such when associated with Yahweh and is simply translated "Lord."

מְגֹאָל הוּא. Pu ptc m s abs √גָּאַל + indep pers pron 3 m s. מְגֹאָל means of "defiled" or "polluted" and functions as a predicate adjective (see note on גָּאַל in 1:7). This is a verbless clause with a predicative usage of the pronoun.

וְנִיבוֹ. *Waw* cop with noun m s constr and 3 m s pronominal suf. נִיבוֹ is a problematic word only occurring here and in Isa 57:19. BDB translates the word as fruit but this translation is problematic in both references (BDB, 626). *BHS* note 12[b–b] proposes omitting the word altogether based on dittography, the presence of אָכְלוֹ that makes the word superfluous, and the absence of this word in the Syriac, Targums, and some ancient Hebrew manuscripts. Stuart also argues that the word should be omitted based upon these reasons (Stuart, 1307). However, although the reading is awkward, emendation is not necessary if the writer is using the word in parallel with אָכְלוֹ.

נִבְזֶה אָכְלוֹ:. Niph ptc m s abs √בָּזָה + noun m s constr with 3 m s pronominal suf. The participle functions as a finite verb in past tense, with אָכְלוֹ as the subject. נִבְזֶה occurs again in the same form in 2:9.

1:13 וַאֲמַרְתֶּם הִנֵּה מַתְּלָאָה וְהִפַּחְתֶּם אוֹתוֹ אָמַר יְהוָה
צְבָאוֹת וַהֲבֵאתֶם גָּזוּל וְאֶת־הַפִּסֵּחַ וְאֶת־הַחוֹלֶה
וַהֲבֵאתֶם אֶת־הַמִּנְחָה הַאֶרְצֶה אוֹתָהּ מִיֶּדְכֶם אָמַר
יְהוָה:

In verse 13, Yahweh continues his accusations against the priest.

וַאֲמַרְתֶּם הִנֵּה מַתְּלָאָה וְהִפַּחְתֶּם אוֹתוֹ אָמַר יְהוָה
צְבָאוֹת. Two temporal clauses joined by a simple conjunction.

וַאֲמַרְתֶּם הִנֵּה מַתְּלָאָה. Qal *weqatal* 3 m pl √אָמַר + demons interj + interrog part with noun f s. This is a dependent, temporal clause. The *weqatal* verb continues the discourse from verse 12. The interjection הִנֵּה heightens the expressed feeling of the next word מַתְּלָאָה.

מַתְּלָאָה. This word consists of the interrogative particle מָה and the noun תְּלָאָה. The dagesh lene in the תּ is the assimilation of the audible ה of מָה into the first letter of the noun (GKC §37*b*). It is a contraction of מָה־תְּלָאָה. This noun is rare, occurring only three other times in the Hebrew Bible: Exod 18:8; Num 20:14; and Lam 3:5. This one word phrase is best translated as words of exasperation "what a weariness!," perhaps showing a boredom of their priestly duties and scorn for their office (Verhoef, 233).

וְהִפַּחְתֶּם אוֹתוֹ. *Waw* cop with Hiph *qatal* 2 m pl √נָפַח + sign of dir obj with 3 m s pronominal suf. The verb נָפַח means to "blow upon" but can mean to "sniff at" as in contempt (BDB, 656). The context suggests that it is an action of contempt, probably an idiom.

Perhaps, the verb here means to breathe hard, as in exasperation. The pronominal suffix on the sign of the direct object refers to שֻׁלְחַן אֲדֹנָי in verse 12. However, Niccacci argues that the direct object is not "the table of the Lord" but God's accusations (Niccacci, 78). This connection seems unlikely given that the immediate context is about the temple offerings.

אָמַר יְהוָה צְבָאוֹת. Prophetic messenger formula. See note in 1:4.

וַהֲבֵאתֶם גָּזוּל וְאֶת־הַפִּסֵּחַ וְאֶת־הַחוֹלֶה וַהֲבֵאתֶם אֶת־הַמִּנְחָה. Declarative clause continuing Yahweh's accusations of the previous clause.

וַהֲבֵאתֶם. *Waw* conj with Hiph *qatal* 3 m pl √בוא. The Hiphil *qatal* has the causative sense and is used here as "bring near" taking on the technical sense of offering in this context (Verhoef, 233).

גָּזוּל וְאֶת־הַפִּסֵּחַ וְאֶת־הַחוֹלֶה. Qal pass ptc m s abs √גָזַל + *waw* cop with sign of dir obj – def art with adj m s + *waw* cop with sign of dir obj – def art with Qal act ptc m s abs √חָלָה. This phrase functions as a substantive chain connected by *waw* copulatives and the sign of the direct object. Hill argues that the *waw* conjunctions are better understood in the alternative sense "or" rather than consecutive sense "and" (Hill, 192). Either interpretation makes sense. The entire chain is the direct object of וַהֲבֵאתֶם. The adjectives parallel types of animals in 1:8, except עִוֵּר "the blind" is missing and has been replaced with גָּזוּל "torn." BDB points out that גָּזוּל probably refers to "being torn away" as in rescued from attack by a wild animal, therefore, the animal is mutilated (BDB, 159–60). *HALOT* translates the term as "unsuitable" (*HALOT*, 186). In any case, the animals described in this phrase are not suitable for human consumption (cf. Lev 7:24; 17:15; 22:8, etc.); how much more are they inappropriate for sacrifice to Yahweh.

וַהֲבֵאתֶם אֶת־הַמִּנְחָה. *Waw* conj with Hiph *qatal* 2 m pl √בוא + sign of dir obj – def art with noun f s. וַהֲבֵאתֶם is repeated here to emphasize the sacrificial act (Verhoef, 233).

‫הָאֶרְצֶה אוֹתָהּ מִיֶּדְכֶם אָמַר יְהוָה:‬ The clause continues the irony found in this oracle in that the interrogative functions as a rhetorical question, one having an emphatic "no" answer, and a declaration of Yahweh's view of the priestly offerings. The question echoes the final declarative clause of 1:10. This parallelism effectively ends this discourse. The two parallel clauses form an envelope construction of verses 10-13 (Hill, 193). The abbreviated messenger formula, ‫אָמַר יְהוָה‬, minus ‫צְבָאוֹת‬, effectively closes the flow of thought. *BHS* note 13ᵉ, along with multiple Hebrew manuscripts, LXX, and Syriac suggest adding ‫צְבָאוֹת‬; however, the omission of the word may have been intentional to break up the monotony of the repetitive messenger formulas.

‫הָאֶרְצֶה‬. Interrog ‫ה‬ with Qal *yiqtol* 1 c s √‫רָצָה‬. The *yiqtol* verb with the interrogative is translated as "shall I accept. . . ."

Malachi 1:14

¹⁴"*Cursed be the deceiver who has a male in his flock and vows [to give it] but sacrificing the blemished to the Lord. For I am a great king," says the Yahweh of hosts, "and my name is feared among the nations.*

‫1:14 וְאָרוּר נוֹכֵל וְיֵשׁ בְּעֶדְרוֹ זָכָר וְנֹדֵר וְזֹבֵחַ מָשְׁחָת‬
‫לַאדֹנָי כִּי מֶלֶךְ גָּדוֹל אָנִי אָמַר יְהוָה צְבָאוֹת וּשְׁמִי‬
‫נוֹרָא בַגּוֹיִם:‬

After presenting accusations against the priests in verses 6-13, Yahweh pronounces judgment against them in the form of a curse. However, Yahweh expands his audience to include laity, those bringing the sacrifices, as well as those who offer them. Although without imperatives, the statement is an emphatic declaration with the sense of a command. Based on the strength of the Qal passive participle, this clause expresses the acme of Yahweh's disgust over the priestly ministry. Yahweh expresses the antitheses of this curse in his declaration in the second half of the verse.

וְאָרוּר נוֹכֵל וְיֵשׁ בְּעֶדְרוֹ זָכָר וְנֹדֵר וְזֹבֵחַ מָשְׁחָת לַאדֹנָי.
A curse declaration.

וְאָרוּר נוֹכֵל. *Waw* cop with Qal pass ptc m s abs √אָרַר + Qal act ptc m s abs √נָכַל. The *waw* conjunction probably should be left untranslated in emphatic clauses such as this one. The Qal passive participle form of אָרוּר is the strongest word for a condemnation in Biblical Hebrew (*TDOT*, 1:411). Although passive, the participle antic- ipates the action (curse rendered) at an unspecified future time (Stuart, 1308–9). אָרוּר is a predicative participle and its position at the begin- ning of the clause adds emphasis. נוֹכֵל is a rare word in the Masoretic Text, occurring only four times (only here in Malachi) and means "one who acts cleverly" or "deceitfully" thus, "a cheat" (GM, 63). The term is anarthrous and applies to all classes of people (Hill, 194).

וְיֵשׁ בְּעֶדְרוֹ זָכָר. *Waw* cop with subst + בְּ prep with noun m s constr and 3 m s pronominal suf + noun m s. The particle יֵשׁ signi- fies ownership, of a זָכָר in this case. The בְּ preposition has a spatial sense, marking a location within an area (WO §11.2.5b). בְּעֶדְרוֹ is the indirect object, זָכָר is the direct object and indicates a male animal from the flock.

וְנֹדֵר וְזֹבֵחַ מָשְׁחָת לַאדֹנָי. Discourse using a participle series.

וְנֹדֵר. *Waw* cop with Qal act ptc m s abs √נָדַר. The *waw* joins two clauses describing related situations. The participle functions as a finite verb in past tense. The subject and object are implied, thus, "he vowed it."

וְזֹבֵחַ מָשְׁחָת לַאדֹנָי. *Waw* advers with Qal act ptc m s abs √זָבַח + Hoph ptc f s abs √שָׁחַת + לְ prep with def art and pr noun. The *waw* adversative indicates that this clause is not what was expected in the previous clause, therefore should be translated "but." However, Hill says the *waw* is a conjunction that indicates the result of the previous action and should be translated "then" (Hill, 195). The Qal parti- ciple functions as a verb of indefinite time, translated as "sacrificing." The Hophal participle מָשְׁחָת only occurs here and in Prov 25:25. The participle has a substantive function and is the direct object,

indicating what is sacrificed. For a discussion of לַאדֹנָי, see note in
1:12. Hill says the "datival *lamed* of interest marks Yahweh as the
deity for whom the action of sacrifice is directed" (Hill, 195).

כִּי מֶלֶךְ גָּדוֹל אָנִי אָמַר יְהֹוָה צְבָאוֹת וּשְׁמִי נוֹרָא בַגּוֹיִם׃.
In the second part of verse 13, the discourse shifts from the faults of
the priests and people to the greatness of Yahweh.

כִּי מֶלֶךְ גָּדוֹל אָנִי. Conj + noun m s + adj m s + indep pers pron
1 c s. כִּי is a conjunction and is a logical marker indicating the beginning of a subordinate clause (WO §39.3.4e). This is a verbless clause.
The phrase מֶלֶךְ גָּדוֹל is predicative with an attributive usage of גָּדוֹל
modifying מֶלֶךְ (Kelley, 53). The reference to Yahweh as the "great
king" may be the writer's allusion to Pss 47:3 and 95:3 (Hill, 195).

אָמַר יְהֹוָה צְבָאוֹת. Prophetic messenger formula, see note in
1:4.

וּשְׁמִי נוֹרָא בַגּוֹיִם׃. *Waw* cop with noun m s constr and 1 c s
pronominal suf + Niph ptc m s abs √יָרֵא + בְּ prep with noun m pl abs.
שְׁמִי is the subject of the clause and בַגּוֹיִם is the indirect object. The בְּ
preposition has a spatial sense, marking location (WO §11.2.5b). The
Niphal participle is temporally ambiguous; however, I have translated
it in the present passive tense "is feared." יָרֵא is a stative verb and usually is translated "fear," but it has the sense of "reverence" (BDB, 431),
something the priests have not been showing Yahweh. This phrase is
reminiscent of verse 11, which states, "my name is great among the
nations," and is antithetical to verse 6, where Yahweh declares the
priests are "despisers of my name." The wording in these three verses
serves as a connector and creates a unified literary panel within the
second oracle (Hill, 196).

Malachi 2:1-9

[1]*"And now this commandment is for you, priests.* [2]*If you do not listen
and you do not set your heart to give honor to my name," says Yahweh of
hosts, "then I will unleash upon you the curse and I will curse your blessings and indeed I will curse it for you are not setting [it] to heart.* [3]*Behold,*

I am rebuking your offspring and I will spread feces upon your faces, the feces of your festival sacrifice, then he will carry you away with it. *⁴Then you will know that I sent to you this commandment in order to continue my covenant with Levi," says Yahweh of hosts.* *⁵"My covenant was with him, life and peace, and I gave them to him [as] an object of reverence and he revered me and he is put in awe before my name.* *⁶Instruction of truth was in his mouth and injustice was not found on his lips, he walked in peace and uprightness with me and he caused many to turn from iniquity.* *⁷For the lips of a priest keep knowledge and they seek instruction from his mouth for he is a messenger of Yahweh of hosts.* *⁸But you, you have turned aside from the way. You have caused many to stumble in the law, you have corrupted the covenant of Levi," says Yahweh of hosts.* *⁹"And indeed I, I am making you despised and humiliated from all people just as you are not keeping my ways and not lifting faces in the law."*

In 2:1-9, the pseudo-dialogue of the previous section of this oracle changes to a monologue, in which Yahweh alone speaks. The courtroom style arguments of 1:6-14 changes to judgment and sentencing in 2:1-9. This half of the second oracle emphasizes obedience and disobedience to the covenant using various forms of the antonyms בָּרַךְ and אָרַר.

2:1 וְעַתָּה אֲלֵיכֶם הַמִּצְוָה הַזֹּאת הַכֹּהֲנִים:

Verse 1 opens the next section of the second oracle and introduces an announcement of judgment. It is a verbless clause.

וְעַתָּה. *Waw* cop with temp adv. The *waw* + adverb serves to mark a transition in discourse (WO §39.3.4f). The discourse turns from habitual past action to present and future action. The adverb separates the previous section with this one. This is the same usage as in 1:9. Since this word begins a new paragraph, the *waw* copulative can remain untranslated. This compound word commonly introduces judgment oracles (Isa 5:5; 16:14; Jer 18:11; 26:13; Hosea 5:7; etc.; Stuart, 1310).

אֲלֵיכֶם. Prep with 2 m pl pronominal suf. This prepositional phrase is the indirect object and is in the emphatic position to signal a return to a focus on the priests.

הַמִּצְוָה הַזֹּאת. Def art with noun f s + def art with demons pron f s. The pronoun is in an attributive relationship with the noun. The word "commandment" here is a special instruction from Yahweh; however, the word has a strong connection with the laws of Torah. Both the word for commandment in verse 1 and the word for instruction in the following verses are an allusion to Torah and its laws, the epitome of priestly responsibility.

הַכֹּהֲנִים. Def art with noun m pl. Vocative usage.

> 2:2　אִם־לֹא תִשְׁמְעוּ וְאִם־לֹא תָשִׂימוּ עַל־לֵב לָתֵת
> כָּבוֹד לִשְׁמִי אָמַר יְהוָה צְבָאוֹת וְשִׁלַּחְתִּי בָכֶם אֶת־
> הַמְּאֵרָה וְאָרוֹתִי אֶת־בִּרְכוֹתֵיכֶם וְגַם אָרוֹתִיהָ כִּי
> אֵינְכֶם שָׂמִים עַל־לֵב׃

BHS note 2ᵃ suggests this verse is a later addition. However, the announcement of a curse (verse 2) followed by explanation of the curse (verse 3) is common to prophetic literature.

אִם־לֹא תִשְׁמְעוּ וְאִם־לֹא תָשִׂימוּ עַל־לֵב לָתֵת כָּבוֹד לִשְׁמִי אָמַר יְהוָה צְבָאוֹת. Two conditional clauses joined by a simple conjunction.

אִם־לֹא תִשְׁמְעוּ. Hypoth part – neg + Qal *yiqtol* 2 m pl √שָׁמַע. Verhoef points out that אִם with a *yiqtol* verb in the protasis is used to express what is possible in the present or future (Verhoef, 238; see GKC §159*q*). אִם־לֹא is negative a particle of contingency marking the protasis of a conditional clause (WO §38.2d). Hill calls it the protasis of a *real conditional clause* of a condition that was fulfilled in the past or capable of being fulfilled in the future (Hill, 197; WO §38.2d). The tense of the verb is future in this verse and has the meaning of "obey."

וְאִם־לֹא תָשִׂימוּ עַל־לֵב. *Waw* cop with hypoth part – neg + Qal *yiqtol* 2 m pl √שִׂים + prep – noun m s. Second verb of the condition. The *waw* copulative connects two verbs of condition. תָשִׂימוּ עַל־לֵב is a common idiom (appearing 28 times in the Hebrew Bible), meaning "pay attention to" and is used twice in this verse. This three-word combination is used several times in prophetic speeches with the intent to bring wayward ones back to a covenant relationship. See Isa 42:25; 57:1; and Jer 12:11 for examples.

לָתֵת כָּבוֹד לִשְׁמִי. לְ prep with Qal inf constr √נָתַן + noun m s + לְ prep with noun m s constr and 1 c s pronominal suf. The לְ preposition + Qal inf constr form a purpose clause. The phrase echoes the question of 1:6, "where is my honor." The לְ preposition of לִשְׁמִי has an allative spatial sense, meaning "in regard to" (WO §11.2.10d).

אָמַר יְהוָה צְבָאוֹת. Prophetic messenger formula, adding authority to the clause.

וְשִׁלַּחְתִּי בָכֶם אֶת־הַמְּאֵרָה וְאָרוֹתִי אֶת־בִּרְכוֹתֵיכֶם. Consequential clause or apodosis of a conditional clause.

וְשִׁלַּחְתִּי בָכֶם. Pi *weqatal* 1 c s √שָׁלַח + בְּ prep with 2 m s pronominal suf. The *waw* relative conjunction represents a simple consequence and should be translated "then" (WO §32.2.1c). Since the phrase states the result of a conditional clause, the *qatal* verb should be translated in present (KD, 645) or future tense (Hill, 171) rather than the typical past as one would expect. The Piel form intensifies the action (indicated as I have it translated "unleash" instead of "send"). בָכֶם is the indirect object. The בְּ preposition has a spatial sense of "on" (WO §11.2.5b).

אֶת־הַמְּאֵרָה. Sign of dir obj – def art with noun f s. הַמְּאֵרָה is a word rarely used in the Hebrew Bible, but appears twice in Malachi (also in 3:9). The noun is a cognate of the verb אָרַר, the word used in the next phrase and the strongest word in Biblical Hebrew for "curse." אָרַר has the sense of judgment. Gordon notes that מְאֵרָה can be associated with poverty, which is the implication in 3:9 (*NIDOT*, 1:526). The inclusion of the definite article, combined with שִׁלַּחְתִּי,

indicates a curse on the order of the curses mentioned in Deuteronomy (cf Deut 28:20). Interestingly, Gordon sees the use of אָרַר in the second oracle as "destabilizing liturgical mockery" or "anti-blessing" that is based upon and antithetical to the use of בָּרַךְ in the Aaronic blessing in Num 6:22-27 (*NIDOT*, 1:525).

וְאָרוֹתִי אֶת־בִּרְכוֹתֵיכֶם. Qal *wᵉqatal* 1 c s √אָרַר + sign of dir obj – noun f pl constr with 2 m pl pronominal suf. A simple *waw* connects אָרוֹתִי with the previous clause as a sign of continued action. Hill identifies the *waw* as a relative *waw* (Hill, 199), as is the *waw* relative with the previous verb. Note that the verbal form of בְּרָכָה (this form is a noun here and is the object of the verb), is an antonym of אָרַר; they are polar opposites. בְּרָכָה has the idea of favored by Yahweh, where as אָרַר indicates a lack of or removal of favor (*NIDOT*, 1:764).

וְגַם אָרוֹתִיהָ כִּי אֵינְכֶם שָׂמִים עַל־לֵב׃. This *qatal* verb with גַם makes this clause an empathic repetition of the previous clause, emphasizing the result as a certainty (opposed to KD, 645).

וְגַם אָרוֹתִיהָ. *Waw* cop with clausal adv + Qal *qatal* 1 c s √אָרַר with 3 f s pronominal suf. The adverb has an emphatic force and can be translated "indeed," marking the beginning of a clause expressing the result of the conditional clause. Waltke and O'Connor say that גַם "can signal a final climax in an exposition and is the only Hebrew adverb that marks a discourse ending" (WO §39.3.4d). The verb in the Qal *qatal* form normally is translated past tense, as many Bibles translate this word (NASB, RSV, NRSV, NIV, etc.). However, the context of the word suggests that the word should be translated in the future, in the sense of immediate impending action, as it is translated in the LXX with καταράσομαι (see Stuart, 1311–12). Although translated in an immediate future sense, the use of the *qatal* has the force of completed action, giving the assurance that the action will occur (GKC §106*m*). The third feminine singular pronominal suffix refers to בִּרְכוֹתֵיכֶם although the word is plural. The suffix is a collective singular. Keil and Delitzsch suggest that the suffix refers to each

particular blessing, and therefore is singular (KD, 645). The LXX
translates בְּרְכוֹתֵיכֶם as singular, εὐλογίαν (see *BHS* note 2ᵇ).

כִּי אֵינְכֶם שָׂמִים עַל־לֵב׃. Part + neg subst with 2 m pl pronominal suf + Qal act ptc m pl abs √שִׂים + prep – noun m s. The כִּי
particle signals a subordinate clause with causal force "because" (WO
§38.4.a). אֵינְכֶם functions as the subject ("you") and verb ("are not")
of this clause, and indicates that the conditions of the clause of the
protasis are not being met. שָׂמִים עַל־לֵב is almost identical to the
same three-word phrase used earlier. See note on this phrase above.

2:3 הִנְנִי גֹעֵר לָכֶם אֶת־הַזֶּרַע וְזֵרִיתִי פֶרֶשׁ עַל־פְּנֵיכֶם
       פֶּרֶשׁ חַגֵּיכֶם וְנָשָׂא אֶתְכֶם אֵלָיו׃

הִנְנִי גֹעֵר לָכֶם אֶת־הַזָּרַע. Independent, declarative clause.

הִנְנִי גֹעֵר. Interj with 1 c s pronominal suf + Qal act ptc m s abs
√גָּעַר. The Qal participle indicates immediate or continuous action.
Given this clause is an announcement of judgment, the action is in
the immediate future, an impending action (WO §37.6d). Since participles do not inherently have a subject, the pronominal suffix on
the interjection functions as the subject. A form of גָּעַר is common
in prophetic language and is synonymous with cursing (see Isa 50:2;
51:20; 54:9; Zech 3:2; etc.).

לָכֶם. Indir obj of גָּעַר. Hill calls the preposition a *lamed* of disadvantage, because the actions is against the recipients of the action
(Hill, 200).

אֶת־הַזֶּרַע. Sign of dir obj – def art with noun m s. *BHS* note
3ᵇ suggests reading "arm" instead of "seed" or "offspring," following
the LXX reading τὸν ὦμον. The emendation is one of pointing only,
since both words have the same consonants. This choice of translation is therefore a theological one. זֶרַע could refer to harvest or one's
children. Blessing the harvest is emphasized in 3:10-11, so זֶרַע as
"harvest" does fit in with broader context. However, the immediate
context is concerning priestly actions so זֶרַע as "harvest" is out of

place. Furthermore, זֶרַע is not used anywhere else in the Hebrew Bible to mean "crops." Translating the word as "arm" has its difficulties too, namely that the consonants in the Masoretic Text are not pointed for this word. However, the arm could be an idiom for the action of priests, that is, they use their arms to offer sacrifices or to give blessings (raising of the arm; see KD, 645). My preference is to retain the Masoretic Text and translate זֶרַע as "offspring" since there is no clear alternative. Whichever the case, the word is the object of Yahweh's judgment.

וְזֵרִיתִי פֶרֶשׁ עַל־פְּנֵיכֶם פֶּרֶשׁ חַגֵּיכֶם וְנָשָׂא אֶתְכֶם אֵלָיו׃ Declarative clause joined to a clause of consequence.

וְזֵרִיתִי. Pi *wᵉqatal* 1 c s √זרה. *Waw* relative with a finite verb following a participle suggests a consequential situation in the immediate future (Hill, 201). The word means "scatter" as in sowing, but here probably has the connotation of "smear" (GM, 45).

פֶרֶשׁ עַל־פְּנֵיכֶם. Noun m s + prep – noun m pl constr with 2 m pl pronominal suf. פֶרֶשׁ refers to the contents of the bowels of sacrificed animals, which the priests were to burn as refuse at a location away from the altar (Exod 29:14; Lev 4:11; 8:17). The phrase is a double entendre in meaning as the act is an act of humiliation and contact with the "unclean" matter makes the priests "unclean" for their priestly duties (Verhoef, 242). פֶרֶשׁ is the direct object. פְּנֵיכֶם has a locational sense (WO §11.2.13).

פֶּרֶשׁ חַגֵּיכֶם. Noun m s constr + noun m pl constr with 2 m pl pronominal suf. The phrase stands in apposition to פֶרֶשׁ and attempts to specify the material from which the first member (פֶּרֶשׁ) is made. *BHS* note 3ᶜ⁻ᶜ suggests this phrase is a later addition.

וְנָשָׂא אֶתְכֶם אֵלָיו. Qal *wᵉqatal* 3 m s √נשׂא + sign of dir obj with 2 m pl pronominal suf + prep with 3 m s pronominal suf. The *waw* relative is a consequential conjunction, translated "then" (WO §32.2.1c). The phrase is problematic because the subject of נָשָׂא is third person. However, this is not an issue if the subject refers to a generic person who carries the פֶּרֶשׁ to the dung pile and if the third singular suffix refers to the place where refuse is tossed and burned (see Verhoef, 242–43). Rather than being a secondary clause (as *BHS* note 3^d–d), the action is the ultimate rejection of the priests, thus making the clause a culmination of thought. Because it is following a consequential clause and because it is a *wᵉqatal* form, the verb should be translated as a nonperfective of impending action, that is, in the future sense.

2:4 וִידַעְתֶּ֗ם כִּ֤י שִׁלַּ֨חְתִּי֙ אֲלֵיכֶ֔ם אֵ֖ת הַמִּצְוָ֣ה הַזֹּ֑את
לִהְי֤וֹת בְּרִיתִי֙ אֶת־לֵוִ֔י אָמַ֖ר יְהוָ֥ה צְבָאֽוֹת׃

Consequential clause. The *waw* relative introduces a conditional clause expressing result and in future time (WO §32.2.3a). It completes the thought began in 2:1.

וִידַעְתֶּ֗ם. Qal *wᵉqatal* 2 m pl √יָדַע. Hill calls this a recognition formula, in that, the priests will have acknowledged Yahweh's judgment (Hill, 203).

כִּ֤י שִׁלַּ֨חְתִּי֙ אֲלֵיכֶ֔ם אֵ֖ת הַמִּצְוָ֣ה הַזֹּ֑את. Subordinate clause.

כִּ֤י שִׁלַּ֨חְתִּי֙ אֲלֵיכֶ֔ם. Clausal adv + Pi *qatal* 1 c s √שָׁלַח + prep with 2 m pl pronominal suf. כִּי has a logical sense and is translated "then" (WO §39.3.4e). The clause expresses recognition of past action so the *qatal* should be translated in its typical past time. The Piel *qatal* takes on a causative sense in this verb thereby emphasizing the source of the commandment—Yahweh.

אֲלֵיכֶ֔ם. The preposition marks a dative, indicating the indirect object (WO §11.2.2a).

אֵ֖ת הַמִּצְוָ֣ה הַזֹּ֑את. Sign of dir obj + def art with noun f s + def art with demons pron f s. The demonstrative pronoun functions attributively.

לִהְי֤וֹת בְּרִיתִי֙ אֶת־לֵוִ֔י. לְ prep and Qal inf constr √הָיָה + noun f s constr with 1 c s pronominal suf + sign of dir obj – prop noun. Although one can easily translate the words, this clause is problematic in meaning. "To be my covenant with Levi" does not make sense in this context. Scholars offer a variety of interpretations but the most probable meaning is to translate the לְ preposition as the marker of a purpose clause ("in order to"), בְּרִיתִי as the direct object of the clause. The infinitive construct לִהְיוֹת functions as a finite verb in a durative sense (see Stuart, 1315–17; WO §36.2.3d), and is translated "to continue." *BHS* note 2:4ᵇ suggests amending the text to the participial form מֶהְיוֹת; however, the infinitive construct form can indicate continuous action so the emendation is not necessary. בְּרִיתִי אֶת־לֵוִי does not occur elsewhere in the Hebrew Bible but the prophet has drawn upon the blessing of Levi in Deut 33:8-11 or the rewarding of Phineas in Num 25:11-13 (see O'Brien, 104–5).

אָמַר יְהוָה צְבָאוֹת׃. Prophetic messenger formula.

2:5   בְּרִיתִי הָיְתָה אִתּוֹ הַחַיִּים וְהַשָּׁלוֹם וָאֶתְּנֵם־לוֹ מוֹרָא
וַיִּירָאֵנִי וּמִפְּנֵי שְׁמִי נִחַת הוּא׃

בְּרִיתִי הָיְתָה אִתּוֹ הַחַיִּים וְהַשָּׁלוֹם. Clarification clause describing בְּרִיתִי of verse 4.

בְּרִיתִי הָיְתָה אִתּוֹ. Noun f s constr with 1 c s pronominal suf + Qal *qatal* 3 f s √הָיָה + prep with 3 m s pronominal suf. בְּרִיתִי is fronted to emphasize the subject. The object of the clause אִתּוֹ refers to Levi in verse 4.

הַחַיִּים וְהַשָּׁלוֹם. Def art with noun m pl + *waw* cop with def art and noun m s. These names are predicate nominatives modifying בְּרִיתִי. הַחַיִּים is a plural noun with a singular meaning "life" (BDB, 313) rather than an adjective (Owens, 934). The definite articles are not translated. The *waw* is a simple conjunction.

וָאֶתְּנֵם־לוֹ מוֹרָא וַיִּירָאֵנִי וּמִפְּנֵי שְׁמִי נִחַת הוּא׃. Clause of clarification describing Yahweh's covenant relationship with Levi.

וָאֶתְּנֵם־לוֹ מוֹרָא. Qal *wayyiqtol* 1 c s √נָתַן with 3 m pl pronominal suf – לְ prep with 3 m s pronominal suf + noun m s. The *wayyiqtol* form expresses the perfective value, continuing the sequence of thought (WO §33.3.1). The לְ preposition is datival, marking the

indirect object (WO §11.2.10d). מוֹרָא, a compound direct object with
the plural pronominal suffix and both referring to בְּרִיתִי, is a noun
derived from the stative verb יָרֵא. It is used rarely in the Hebrew Bible,
occurring only twelve times, including here and in 1:6. מוֹרָא in 2:5
ideologically parallels its usage 1:6 where Yahweh says he is not receiving the "fear" he deserves and it parallels the verb in the next phrase.

וַיִּירָאֵנִי. Qal *wayyiqtol* 3 m s √יָרֵא with 1 c s pronominal suf. The
wayyiqtol verb signifies an event of logical sequence (WO §33.3.1d;
Hill, 207).

וּמִפְּנֵי שְׁמִי נִחַת הוּא. *Waw* cop with מִן prep and noun m pl
constr + noun m s constr with 1 c s pronominal suf + Niph *qatal* 3 m s
√חָתַת + indep pers pron. The *waw* is conjunctive, joining this phase
with the previous one. מִפְּנֵי is a spatial idiom meaning "before" but
literally means "from the faces of." The phrase מִפְּנֵי שְׁמִי is placed at
the beginning of the phrase for emphasis. The Niphal form of חָתַת
means "put in awe" rather than "be shattered" (BDB, 369; see Hill,
208). Hill notes that חָתַת and יָרֵא often occur in synonymous parallelism (Hill, 208). The personal pronoun הוּא functions as the subject
of the clause and is emphatic since the verb carries the pronoun. Hill
says הוּא provides logical contrast between the Levi and the priests
(Hill, 208).

2:6   תּוֹרַת אֱמֶת הָיְתָה בְּפִיהוּ וְעַוְלָה לֹא־נִמְצָא בִשְׂפָתָיו
בְּשָׁלוֹם וּבְמִישׁוֹר הָלַךְ אִתִּי וְרַבִּים הֵשִׁיב מֵעָוֺן׃

Verse 6 continues clarifying Yahweh's covenant with Levi in verse
4. The verse is composed of three clauses that clarify Yahweh's relationship with Levi. These clauses alternate positive/negative/positive
but are synonymously parallel in thought.

תּוֹרַת אֱמֶת הָיְתָה בְּפִיהוּ וְעַוְלָה לֹא־נִמְצָא בִשְׂפָתָיו.
Clause of description, clarifying the Levi's disposition.

תּוֹרַת אֱמֶת. Noun f s constr + noun f s. This genitival phrase is
the subject of the clause, a unique phrase in the Hebrew Bible. תּוֹרַת

means "instruction" as in oral instruction of priestly duty rather than the Sinai covenant (Stuart, 1320) although it could be an intended double entendre reflecting both meanings. Enns says תּוֹרָה defines a "divine standard of conduct for God's people" (*NIDOT*, 4:893), which is implied here. The word occurs five times in Malachi (2:6, 7, 8, 9; and 3:22).

הָיְתָה. Qal *qatal* 3 f s √הָיָה.

בְּפִיהוּ. בְּ prep with noun m s constr and 3 m s pronominal suf. This is a prepositional phrase with a spatial function, literally meaning "in his mouth," that forms an idiom for one's speech.

וְעַוְלָה לֹא־נִמְצָא בִשְׂפָתָיו. *Waw* cop with noun f s + neg – Niph *qatal* 3 m s √מָצָא + בְּ prep with noun f dual constr and 3 m s pronominal suf. This is a negative clause paralleling the previous positive clause, joined together by a *waw* copulative. The subject/verb/object word order emphasizes the subject. וְעַוְלָה is in opposition to בְּפִיהוּ and בִשְׂפָתָיו is synonymously paralleled with תּוֹרַת אֱמֶת.

בְּשָׁלוֹם וּבְמִישׁוֹר הָלַךְ אִתִּי. Final clause of clarification in verse 6. This clause is stated positively, but is parallel to the previous negative clause.

בְּשָׁלוֹם וּבְמִישׁוֹר. בְּ prep with noun m s + *waw* cop with בְּ prep and noun m s. The בְּ preposition has a spatial sense to mark location (WO §11.2.5b; Hill, 208). The two nouns, joined by a simple conjunction, describe the state of the subject (the pronoun for Levi). מִישׁוֹר means "level place" but has the connotation of "uprightness" (BDB, 449).

הָלַךְ אִתִּי. Qal *qatal* 3 m s √הָלַךְ + prep with 1 c s pronominal suf. This phrase is an idiom meaning obedience and connotes a close relationship with Yahweh (Verhoef, 248).

וְרַבִּים הֵשִׁיב מֵעָוֹן׃. This is a clause with a logical or sequential sense expressing result due to the action of the previous clause. The subject/verb/object arrangement emphasizes the subject.

וְרַבִּים. *Waw* cop with adj m pl. The adjective רַבִּים functions as nonspecific substantive. Hill suggests that the adjective refers to lay members (Hill, 209–10). However, in the context of Malachi, רַבִּים probably refers to the ones who bring offerings and the ones who listen to the priests' teachings, i.e., the general population.

הֵשִׁיב מֵעָוֹן. Hiph *qatal* 3 m s √שׁוּב + מִן prep with noun m s. The Hiphil verb maintains the typical Hiphil causative sense. The preposition מִן has an ablative sense, indicating movement away from an object (WO §11.2.11b).

2:7 כִּי־שִׂפְתֵי כֹהֵן יִשְׁמְרוּ־דַעַת וְתוֹרָה יְבַקְשׁוּ מִפִּיהוּ כִּי מַלְאַךְ יְהוָה־צְבָאוֹת הוּא:

BHS and others suggest this verse is a later addition to the text because it restates what has already been said in verse 6 (see *BHS*, note 7ᵃ). For a discussion on verse 7 as a later addition, see Verhoef, 249.

כִּי־שִׂפְתֵי כֹהֵן יִשְׁמְרוּ־דַעַת. Part – noun m pl constr + noun m s + Qal *yiqtol* 3 m pl √שָׂפַת – noun f s. The particle כִּי begins the subordinate clause and functions as a conjunctive adverb. However, כִּי may be emphatic here and translated "surely" or "indeed" (Hill, 171, 210). The clause has a subject/verb/object order, emphasizing the subject.

שִׂפְתֵי כֹהֵן. Construct genitival phrase, subject of יִשְׁמְרוּ. The noun כֹהֵן is collective singular, representing all priests. Waltke and O'Connor call it a generic noun of class (WO §13.8b).

יִשְׁמְרוּ. Some scholars translate the *yiqtol* verb as a potential imperfect, in the sense of "ought" or "should" (Smith, 309; GM, 45). However, it has the sense of a present tense, repetitive action rather than a future obligation (Hill, 210–11). The meaning of the verb has the sense of keeping as in preserving.

דַעַת. Dir obj of יִשְׁמְרוּ. The *maqqef* strengthens the tie between the verb and the object.

וְתוֹרָה יְבַקְשׁוּ מִפִּיהוּ. Parallel clause to the previous one and linked by a *waw* copulative. The clause has an object/verb/indirect object order, thus emphasizing the object. The subject is the verbal pronoun and refers to רַבִּים in verse 6 (and verse 8).

וְתוֹרָה. *Waw* cop with noun f s. Dir obj of יְבַקְשׁוּ. The emphatic position of תוֹרָה parallels it with דַעַת. Together with the verbs, they make an A/B//B′/A′ chiasm, further emphasizing "knowledge" and "instruction."

יְבַקְשׁוּ מִפִּיהוּ. Pi *yiqtol* 3 m pl √בָקַשׁ + prep with noun m s constr and 3 m s pronominal suf. The verb continues the sense of the verb of the previous phrase. Hill says that יְבַקְשׁוּ usually is translated as nonperfective of deliberation expressing what ought to be. He suggests translating it as "should seek" (Hill, 212; WO §31.4f). The מִן preposition on מִפִּיהוּ has the sense of location (WO §11.2.11b).

כִּי מַלְאַךְ יְהוָה־צְבָאוֹת הוּא:. Logical or causal clause, concluding a sequence. This is a verbless clause with the predicative usage of the personal pronoun (Kelley, 53). This clause is the climatic conclusion of verses 5-7. Hill calls the clause one of classification (Hill, 213).

כִּי. Clausal adverb indicating result or logical conclusion.

מַלְאַךְ יְהוָה־צְבָאוֹת הוּא. Noun m s + divine title + indep pers pron. This is the only occurrence of מַלְאַךְ יְהוָה־צְבָאוֹת in the Hebrew Bible and the only reference to a priest as a messenger. מַלְאַךְ is usually a term applied to a prophet. On the implications of this phrase for interpreting the pericope, see Hill, 212–13. הוּא is the subject of the clause.

2:8 וְאַתֶּם סַרְתֶּם מִן־הַדֶּרֶךְ הִכְשַׁלְתֶּם רַבִּים בַּתּוֹרָה
שִׁחַתֶּם בְּרִית הַלֵּוִי אָמַר יְהוָה צְבָאוֹת:

Verse 8 shifts the dialogue from discussion of the ideal priest to the present state of the priesthood. The disjunctive *waw* signals the beginning of a clause of contrast. The contrast of verse 8 is with verse 6. The verse has three clauses that build on the emphatic use of the personal pronoun וְאַתֶּם at the beginning of the verse. The lack of *waw* conjunctions between the clauses heightens the tension and urgency due to the contrasting nature of what Yahweh expects and what the priests are doing.

וְאַתֶּם֩ סַרְתֶּ֨ם מִן־הַדֶּ֜רֶךְ. Clause of contrast, in opposition to the previous verse.

וְאַתֶּם֩. *Waw* cop with indep pers pron 2 m pl. The coordinating *waw* prefixed to a nonverbal form is disjunctive and should be translated "but" (WO §39.2.3a). Stuart calls the וְ and אַתֶּם combination a nonconsecutive syntax (Stuart, 1321). The personal pronoun beginning the clause emphasizes the pronoun thereby heightening the contrast between the current priests and the ideal ones.

סַרְתֶּם. Qal *qatal* 2 m pl √סור. The *qatal* verb indicates past action that continues into the present. This verb is parallel to שׁוּב in verse 6 but the two verbs indicate opposite directions of movement.

מִן־הַדֶּרֶךְ. Prep – def art with noun m s. The preposition has an ablative usage, having the sense of moving away. The definite noun הַדֶּרֶךְ echoes covenant language and is idiomatic of one who keeps Yahweh's instruction. This phrase, including the verb, is used similarly to here in Exod 32:8; Deut 11:28; 31:29; etc., and denotes those who turn away from Yahweh.

הִכְשַׁלְתֶּם רַבִּים בַּתּוֹרָה. The subject of the clause carries over from the previous clause and the lack of a conjunction here stresses the continuity. The clause indicates the result of the priests' offense. These clauses have an accusatory force.

הִכְשַׁלְתֶּם. Hi *qatal* 2 m pl √כָּשַׁל. The Hiphil verb is translated in its normal causative sense, keeping the past tense action that continues into the present of the previous verb.

רַבִּים. Adj m pl abs. Dir obj of הִכְשַׁלְתֶּם. The adjective רַבִּים functions as a nonspecific substantive. The word here is an echo of the same term in verse 6 (see note in verse 6) and refers to the same people.

בַּתּוֹרָֽה. בְּ prep with def art and noun f s. Indir obj of הִכְשַׁלְתֶּם. The בְּ preposition may be translated as a circumstance of agents (WO §11.2.5d) where the preposition is translated "by." If "by" is the meaning of the preposition, then תּוֹרָה refers to the priests' instruction (Verhoef, 236; GM 45; Smith, 309). However, the בְּ preposition can be translated adversatively in the sense of "against" or "over" (Hill, 171; KD, 647; Niccacci, 65). In this case, תּוֹרָה refers to the Torah or Law, particularly given that the noun is definite. Stuart, following the second understanding of the usage of the preposition, perhaps offers the best rendering by translating it "in regards to" (Stuart, 1319). Furthermore, since the first and third clauses refer to Yahweh's covenant, understanding תּוֹרָה as "law" rather than priestly "instruction" seems preferable.

שִׁחַתֶּם בְּרִית הַלֵּוִי אָמַר יְהוָה צְבָאֽוֹת: This is the final clause of accusation of this series. This clause echoes the wording of verse 4 and makes a fitting conclusion to Yahweh's case against the priests.

שִׁחַתֶּם בְּרִית הַלֵּוִי. Pi *qatal* 3 m pl √שׁחת + noun f s constr + def art with prop noun. The construct phrase is an attribute genitive (WO §9.5.3b). The phrase closes the thought on the covenant of Levi began in verse 4. The presence of the definite article on הַלֵּוִי may indicate that the name is not for a particular person but for a group of persons—the Levites (Hill, 216). However, Stuart argues that the phrase here and the similar one in verse 4 are identical in meaning, i.e., "Levi" (Stuart, 1322–23). בְּרִית הַלֵּוִי probably refers the Mosaic covenant, especially when used with תּוֹרָה. This is the suzerainty agreement between Yahweh and Israel.

אָמַר יְהוָה צְבָאוֹת. Prophetic messenger formula. See note in 1:4.

2:9   וְגַם־אֲנִי נָתַתִּי אֶתְכֶם נִבְזִים וּשְׁפָלִים לְכָל־הָעָם
כְּפִי אֲשֶׁר אֵינְכֶם שֹׁמְרִים אֶת־דְּרָכַי וְנֹשְׂאִים פָּנִים
בַּתּוֹרָֽה:

Verse 9 is the conclusion of the second oracle and is Yahweh's statement of punishment for the priests.

וְגַם־אָנִי נָתַתִּי אֶתְכֶם נִבְזִים וּשְׁפָלִים לְכָל־הָעָם. The
coordinating conjunction connects this clause with the previous verse.

וְגַם־אָנִי. *Waw* conjunction with adv – indep pers pron 1 c s. The
waw is disjunctive, contrasting the priests' action against Yahweh's
actions (Stuart, 1323). The combination גַּם־אָנִי is an emphatic introduction to the clause. The adverb גַּם followed by a personal pronoun,
as in this instance, can be emphatic and "signal a final climax in an
exposition" (WO §39.3.4d). In this case, the adverb is translated
"indeed." The personal pronoun is the subject of the clause and is
doubly emphasized first by its presence and second by its placement
before the verb. Waltke and O'Connor say this construction indicates
self-assertion, thus has emphasis on the pronoun (WO §16.3.2e).

נָתַתִּי. Qal *qatal* 1 c s √נָתַן. The *qatal* verb describes a pending
action, a consequence of the priests' actions in the previous verses. It
has the meaning of "make" rather than the more frequent "give."

אֶתְכֶם. Sign of dir obj with 2 m pl pronominal suf. Direct object
of נָתַתִּי.

נִבְזִים וּשְׁפָלִים. Niph ptc m pl abs √בָּזָה + *waw* cop with adj
m pl. The participle and adjective modify the object. The participle
נִבְזִים effectively closes the oracle by its antithetical parallel usage here
in conjunction with its use in 1:6, where it opens the oracle (see note
on בָּזָה in 1:6). The priests despised Yahweh (1:6) and now the priests
themselves will be despised (2:9), a reversal of fortune. This parallel
thought, with נֹשְׂאִים פָּנִים below, creates an envelope of thought
within the oracle.

לְכָל־הָעָם. Prepositional phrase. Indir obj of נָתַתִּי. The לְ
preposition has a spatial sense and marks the goal of the verb (WO
§11.2.10d). The noun is singular; however, *BHS* note 9ᵃ proposes
reading the word as plural following multiple Hebrew manuscripts,
LXX, and Vulgate. The choice of singular or plural affects translation. If the word is accepted as singular, "the people" refer to people

of Judah who bring sacrifices to the priests. If the word is plural, then "the people" include people of other nations.

כְּפִּי אֲשֶׁר אֵינְכֶם שֹׁמְרִים אֶת־דְּרָכַי. This is a logical sequence clause showing cause.

כְּפִּי אֲשֶׁר. כְּ prep with noun m s constr + part of relation. This combination is an idiomatic conjunction meaning "in as much as" (*CHAL*, 289). The idiom only occurs here in the Hebrew Bible (BDB, 805).

אֵינְכֶם שֹׁמְרִים. Neg subst constr with 2 m pl pronominal suf + Qal act ptc m pl abs √שָׁמַר. The phrase uses a negative substantive with a participle to state an ongoing negative action. The pronominal suffix is the subject of the clause. שֹׁמְרִים has the meaning of "obedience" and is frequently used in reference to "keeping" Yahweh's law, especially in combination with דֶּרֶךְ.

אֶת־דְּרָכַי. Sign of dir obj – noun m pl constr with 1 c s pronominal suf.

וְנֹשְׂאִים פָּנִים בַּתּוֹרָה׃. This is a conjunctive clause displaying the priests' behavior. The negation from the previous clause continues into this one.

וְנֹשְׂאִים פָּנִים. *Waw* conj with Qal act ptc m pl abs √נָשָׂא + noun m pl. The conjunctive *waw* begins a participial clause of present action. The participle and noun, meaning "lifting up faces," is an idiom meaning "to show favor" (Stuart, 1324). Glazier-McDonald argues that the phrase means "to regard" or "consider." She bases her argument upon similar wording in Prov 6:35 (GM, 73). However, the wording of Prov 6:35 is not identical to this phrase and the more common usage of these words is "to show favor." Hill proposes that the conjunction is a *waw* copulative and that it joins this clause with the previous one and both share the same subject, אֵינְכֶם. Thus, he translates the clause "[you are not] acting graciously in [matters of] Torah" (Hill, 171, 217–18). In this case, the phrase נֹשְׂאִים פָּנִים is an idiom meaning "act graciously" by showing favor. This interpretation makes the most sense. The writer is using this phrase in apposition to the question in 1:9, which has similar wording, "Will [Yahweh] lift up your faces?" Therefore, the phrase וְנֹשְׂאִים פָּנִים serves as an envelope to 1:9 and makes a fitting closing to the second oracle.

בַּתּוֹרָה. Prep בְּ with def art and noun f s. בַּתּוֹרָה is the indirect object of וְנֹשְׂאִים. See note on בַּתּוֹרָה in 2:8.

Third Oracle: Sinful Community (2:10-16)

Malachi 2:10-16

¹⁰"Does not all of us have one father? Did not God create us? Why do we act treacherously with one another to pollute the covenant of our fathers? ¹¹Judah has acted treacherously and an abomination has been done in Israel and in Jerusalem for Judah has profaned the holiness of Yahweh which he loved, and he married the daughter of a foreign god. ¹²May Yahweh cut off the man who one wakes and who responds from the tents of Jacob even the one who brings an offering to Yahweh of hosts. ¹³And this is a second thing you do, covering with tears the altar of Yahweh, weeping and groaning, because there is no one anymore looking to the offering and taking pleasure from your hand. ¹⁴But you say, 'Why is that?' Because Yahweh is a witness between you and between the wife of your youth which you acted treacherously against her for she [was] your companion and the wife of your covenant. ¹⁵But has no one done [this thing] and [has] a remainder of a spirit in him? And what is the one seeking—offspring of God? Then you take heed in your spirit and let no one act treacherously against the wife of your youth. ¹⁶For he hates divorce" says Yahweh, God of Israel "and he covered over violence with his garment," says Yahweh of hosts. "Then you take heed in your spirit and do not act treacherously."

The third oracle can be divided into two parts 10-12 and 13-16. Each part reflects a complaint Yahweh has with the priests. The verb בָּגַד appears frequently in this pericope, and is central to the complaints found in each section. The writer returns to using rhetorical questions in his prophetic disputation as he did in the first oracle and in the first part of the second oracle. Except for a quotation of Yahweh in verse 16, the third oracle is presented from the perspective of the prophet, which differs from the previous oracle that is presented from the perspective of Yahweh. Covenant and the metaphor of marriage are linked here and in Hosea, where marriage fidelity is symbolic of covenant fidelity (*NIDOT*, 1:751).

Key Words					
אָהַב	אֵשֶׁת נְעוּרֶיךָ	בָּגַד	בָּרָא	שָׂנֵא	תּוֹעֵבָה

2:10 הֲלוֹא אָב אֶחָד לְכֻלָּנוּ הֲלוֹא אֵל אֶחָד בְּרָאָנוּ מַדּוּעַ
נִבְגַּד אִישׁ בְּאָחִיו לְחַלֵּל בְּרִית אֲבֹתֵינוּ:

Verse 10 begins the third oracle with three rhetorical questions. The first two are meant to be answered positively (with a "yes" as implied by context). These clauses have parallel grammatical construction except for the last word. This parallel construction ties these two clauses together and emphasizes their unity of thought. Their purpose is to set up the third question, which requires a longer answer and is Yahweh's real concern.

הֲלוֹא אָב אֶחָד לְכֻלָּנוּ. Interrogative verbless clause. Waltke and O'Connor call this a question of fact (WO §18.1c).

הֲלוֹא. Interrog part with neg adv. This combination is emphatic (Stuart, 1327). Hill notes the interrogative "identifies a rhetorical question, intended 'to give information with passion'" (Hill, 224). Merwe points out that הֲלוֹא marks a rhetorical question that cannot be easily contested, as is the case here (MNK, 322).

אָב אֶחָד. Noun m s + adj m s. This is an attributive relationship with the adjective modifying the noun.

לְכֻלָּנוּ. לְ prep with noun m s constr and 1 c pl pronominal suf. Predicate of the clause. The לְ preposition expresses possession (WO §11.2.10d). The substantive כֹּל is a genitive of quantity. The pronoun of the suffix refers to the people of Judah (Hill, 224).

הֲלוֹא אֵל אֶחָד בְּרָאָנוּ. Negative interrogative clause.

הֲלוֹא. See note on הֲלוֹא above.

אֵל אֶחָד. Noun m s + adj m s. These words are synonymously paralleled with אָב אֶחָד. This is the only occurrence of this word combination in the Hebrew Bible. The phase is not about the unity of God but rather about gaining the people's unity of purpose, which is founded in God alone. The phrase reflects Deut 6:4, the verse that epitomizes Yahweh.

בְּרָאָנוּ. Qal, *qatal* 3 m s √בָּרָא with 1 c pl pronominal suf. The *qatal* verb is translated in past tense and of completed action. בָּרָא is used in association with God only, thus only God "creates." Ringgren says בָּרָא is more than the act of creating but also includes election. Yahweh "made" (עָשָׂה) the earth but "created" (בָּרָא) man (Isa 43:12) indicating that man was the most important work of creation. Furthermore, Isa 43:1, 7, 15 indicates God created only Israel among the nations, giving Israel elected status. Ringgren says Israel's election is included in the meaning here (*TDOT*, 2:247).

מַדּוּעַ נִבְגַּד אִישׁ בְּאָחִיו לְחַלֵּל בְּרִית אֲבֹתֵינוּ׃ Independent, interrogative clause.

מַדּוּעַ. Interrog part. This particle is a combination of the interrogative מָה and the Qal passive participle of יָדַע. The combination means "why" in the sense of "for what reason" (WO §18, note 17). Here, it introduces a question of circumstance.

נִבְגַּד. Qal *yiqtol* 1 c pl √בָּגַד. The word means to "act treacherously" but here refers to faithless behavior as in a relationship (in marriage and in covenant relationship; GM, 85). In this clause, the faithlessness is toward Yahweh, but in the second part of the oracle, the faithlessness is toward one's wife. Wakely notes that the most frequent object of בָּגַד is God (*NIDOT*, 1:586). Furthermore, Wakely says that marriage symbolism in prophetic literature is used to portray the relationship of Yahweh with his people, especially in terms of betrayal and treachery (*NIDOT*, 1:586–87); which is the case in this pericope. The pointing of the text is identical to a Niphal *qatal* 3 m s form. The text allows for translating the verb in this clause as a third masculine singular form, with אִישׁ as the subject—"why does a man act treacherously against his brother?" However, נִבְגַּד does not occur in the Niphal stem (BDB, 93). This, combined with the frequent first common plural pronominal suffixes in this verse, makes this translation unlikely. בָּגַד also occurs in verses 11, 14, 15, and 16 in the third oracle.

אִישׁ בְּאָחִיו. Noun m s + בְּ prep with noun m s constr and 3 m s pronominal suf. This phrase literally means "a man with his brother," but it is an idiom meaning "with one another." This phrase appears frequently in the Hebrew Bible indicating a reciprocal relationship (BDB, 946). The בְּ preposition has an adversarial sense (Hill, 227).

לְחַלֵּל. Pi inf constr √חלל. Hill points out that the combination of נִבְגַּד, לְחַלֵּל, and בְּרִית "indicates behavior that violates Yahweh's covenant, a breach of contract meriting divine punishment" (Hill, 227). לְחַלֵּל is in parallel with נִבְגַּד and appears in parallel construction again in verse 11. The infinitive construct identifies the purpose of action of the finite verb נִבְגַּד (MNK, 155).

בְּרִית אֲבֹתֵינוּ. Noun f s constr + noun m pl constr with 1 c pl pronominal suf. The phrase is the direct object of לְחַלֵּל. The construct relationship reflects the relationship of possession. This phrase in unique in the prophetic books to this occurrence in Malachi and has a near parallel only in Deut 4:31, which says "covenant with your fathers."

2:11 בָּגְדָה יְהוּדָה וְתוֹעֵבָה נֶעֶשְׂתָה בְיִשְׂרָאֵל וּבִירוּשָׁלָ͏ם
כִּי | חִלֵּל יְהוּדָה קֹדֶשׁ יְהוָה אֲשֶׁר אָהֵב וּבָעַל בַּת־
אֵל נֵכָר׃

Some scholars think that 2:11-13a are later additions (see Fohrer, 470). They base this argument upon the fact that these verses present Yahweh in third person rather than first person as in the previous and following verses. Also, one can read 2:10 then skip to 2:13b without losing continuity of thought. However, most scholars see 2:11-13a as an integral part of the prophet's message and hold it to be original to the text (see Merrill, 381). The first half of the verse 10 has an A/B/A′/B′ synonymous parallel pattern—"act treacherously," "Judah," "abomination done," "in Israel and in Jerusalem." The second half of the verse expounds on the first half.

בָּגְדָה יְהוּדָה וְתוֹעֵבָה נֶעֶשְׂתָה בְיִשְׂרָאֵל וּבִירוּשָׁלָ͏ִם.
Independent, declarative clause.

בָּגְדָה יְהוּדָה. Qal *qatal* 3 f s √בָּגַד + pr noun. Note that "Judah" is a feminine noun here but is masculine in its next usage in this verse. Stuart calls this a "merism by which the entire population, male and female, is indicated" (Stuart, 1331). However, some country names, as Judah and Edom, can appear as either masculine or feminine. Glazier-McDonald suggests that "Judah" in the feminine refers to the name of the country while "Judah" in the masculine refers to the people within the nation (GM, 89).

וְתוֹעֵבָה נֶעֶשְׂתָה. *Waw* cop with noun f s + Niph *qatal* 3 f s √עָשָׂה. The *waw* copulative is conjunctive, joining the two parallel phrases. The noun תוֹעֵבָה is an important legal term in Deuteronomy (e.g., Deut 7:26; 12:31; 13:15; 14:3; and 24:4) and the term here continues to echo Deuteronomy. Grisanti says that occurrences of the word תוֹעֵבָה has the covenant as a backdrop in the Pentateuch, and in historical and prophetic material. The "detestable" thing is offensive to Yahweh and constitutes a threat to the existence of Israel (*NIDOT*, 4:315). Furthermore, תוֹעֵבָה occurs 43 times in Ezekiel as a comprehensive term for cultic impurity (*NIDOT*, 4:317). It functions the same way here. The phrase תוֹעֵבָה נֶעֶשְׂתָה probably should be read as a unit in parallel with בָּגְדָה. The noun תוֹעֵבָה is singular but probably is a collective singular rather than representing a single offense.

בְיִשְׂרָאֵל וּבִירוּשָׁלָ͏ִם. בְּ prep with pr noun + *waw* cop with בְּ prep and pr noun. Two synonymously paralleled prepositional phrases placed between two occurrences of the word "Judah" emphasize the covenant people, which has a focus in Jerusalem (the location of the temple). The בְּ prepositions are locative or spatial but are an all-inclusive indication of the people who dwell in their realm, i.e., the people the covenant (WO §11.2.5b). *BHS* note 11[b] suggests deleting וּבְיִשְׂרָאֵל but the term nicely fits into its parallel context here and with post-exilic thought. (For a more detailed discussion, see Hill, 229–30; and Verhoef, 268.)

כִּי חִלֵּל יְהוּדָה קֹדֶשׁ יְהוָה אֲשֶׁר אָהֵב. Subordinate clause.

כִּי חִלֵּל יְהוּדָה. Conj + Pi *qatal* 3 m s √חָלַל + pr noun. כִּי is a subordinate conjunction, opening a clause that functions epexegetically. חִלֵּל is in parallel in meaning to בְּגְדָה (see note above in 2:10).

קֹדֶשׁ יְהוָה. Noun m s constr + pr noun. The genitival phrase literally means "the holiness of Yahweh." The word may refer to things or persons ceremonially clean (BDB, 872). Many scholars translate the word to mean "sanctuary" (as GM, 82; Smith, 319; KD, 649). However, the word probably has a broader connotation here meaning everything set apart for Yahweh, including the temple, the covenant people, and the priests (as with Hill, 221). Stuart translates the word as "sanctuary" (Stuart, 1326) but unexpectedly defines the term to mean Yahweh's people (Stuart, 1332), which is confusing (as does Verhoef, 262, 268–69).

אֲשֶׁר אָהֵב. Rel pron + Qal *qatal* 3 m s √אָהֵב. The relative pronoun is conjunctive and introduces a dependent causal clause. The subject of אָהֵב is יְהוָה if קֹדֶשׁ יְהוָה is the object of Yahweh's love, which seems most probable. For a discussion of אָהֵב, see note in 1:2.

וּבָעַל בַּת־אֵל נֵכָר׃. *Waw* cop with Qal *qatal* 3 m s √בָּעַל + noun f s constr – noun m s + noun m s. The *waw* is rendered conjunctive here since this clause is paralleled to the previous כִּי clause. The clause gives details as to how Judah has profaned the holiness of Yahweh. The pronoun of the verb refers to יְהוּדָה. The verb בָּעַל is an infrequent word (occurring 7 times in the Hebrew Bible; BDB, 127) and is used only here in the Book of the Twelve. This phrase is probably idiomatic referring to mixed marriages.

בַּת־אֵל נֵכָר. Dir obj of בָּעַל. The phrase literally means "a daughter of a god of a foreigner;" however, it is usually translated as an attributive phrase "a daughter of a foreign god." Some scholars believe this is a reference to foreign women while others read it as a goddess (see GM, 91–93, for a discussion on the differing views). Most likely, בַּת is antithetically paralleled to אָב in the first question in 2:10. The people of Judah have one father in Yahweh אָב אֶחָד but they are marrying daughters that are of a foreign god אֵל נֵכָר (GM, 92–93).

2:12 יַכְרֵת יְהוָה לָאִישׁ אֲשֶׁר יַעֲשֶׂנָּה עֵר וְעֹנֶה מֵאָהֳלֵי יַעֲקֹב וּמַגִּישׁ מִנְחָה לַיהוָה צְבָאוֹת:

יַכְרֵת יְהוָה לָאִישׁ. Hiph *yiqtol* 3 m s √כָּרַת + pr noun + לְ prep with def art and noun m s. This is a jussive form of the verb כָּרַת and should be translated "may he cut off." Waltke and O'Connor call the function of the jussive as used here as malediction (a curse or imprecation, WO §34.3c). Petersen calls this an impersonal curse formulation and cites similar examples found in Pss 12:3 and 109:15 (Petersen, 200).

יְהוָה. Subject of יַכְרֵת.

לָאִישׁ. Dir obj of יַכְרֵת. The לְ preposition has accusative function, governing the direct object (WO §11.4.1b). אִישׁ is definite and refers to specific men, probably those who have married the foreign women mentioned in 2:11.

אֲשֶׁר יַעֲשֶׂנָּה עֵר וְעֹנֶה מֵאָהֳלֵי יַעֲקֹב. Dependent relative clause describing the actions of אִישׁ, thereby limiting the noun. כָּרַת followed by the מִן preposition are a common combination found in the Hebrew Bible. This clause continues the thought of "may Yahweh cut off . . ." in the previous clause.

אֲשֶׁר יַעֲשֶׂנָּה. Rel pron + Qal *yiqtol* 3 m s √עָשָׂה with 3 f s pronominal suf. This verb is a nonperfective denoting habitual action without a specific tense or time value association (WO §31.3e). In other words, the action occurs repeatedly.

עֵר וְעֹנֶה. Qal act ptc m s abs √עוּר + *waw* cop with Qal act ptc m s abs √עָנָה. This word pair is enigmatic. A Hebrew manuscript, a Qumran Hebrew text (4QXIIa), and the LXX emend עֵר to עֵד meaning "witness" (see *BHS* note 11/12ᶜ). Following this suggestion, the phrase is translated "a witness and one who answers," making the words synonymously paralleled and giving the phrase legal connotations (also Hill, 221). However, many scholars do not agree with emending the text. Since the words represent opposite actions (action and reaction), many scholars suggest that the phrase is idiomatic, a proverbial expression meaning "everyone" (see Petersen, 194; Verhoef, 262). Keil and Delitzsch and Niccacci simply translate the phrase literally (KD, 649; Niccacci, 65), with Keil and Delitzsch associating the participles to two groups of people (wakers and answerers) while Niccacci associates the two actions to the same persons. Glazier-McDonald associates the terms to sexual practices translating the phrase "one who is aroused (from sexual inactivity, i.e., the aroused one) and the lover" (GM, 94–99). Although no clear solution presents itself, the best translation seems to be that of an idiom, a merismus, suggesting the notion of totality meaning "everyone" (Stuart, 1334).

מֵאָהֳלֵי יַעֲקֹב. מִן prep with noun m pl constr + pr noun. Indir obj of יַכְרֵת. The מִן preposition has the sense separation. אָהֳלֵי יַעֲקֹב is an idiomatic reference to the Israelite (Judahite) community. This phrase also occurs in Num 24:5 and Jer 30:18.

וּמַגִּישׁ מִנְחָה לַיהוָה צְבָאוֹת: Dependent relative clause further describing אִישׁ.

וּמַגִּישׁ מִנְחָה. *Waw* cop with Hiph ptc m s abs √נָגַשׁ + noun f s. The *waw* conjunction can be interpreted as a coordinating conjunction that joins this clause with the previous one. However, Hill suggests translating it as an emphatic *waw* as "even" (Hill, 236). This makes sense in that this phrase further distinguishes persons from "the tents of Jacob."

לַיהוָה צְבָאוֹת. Indir obj of וּמַגִּישׁ. The לְ preposition has a terminative sense when it follows a verb of motion (WO §11.2.10b).

Although not the messenger formula, the use of the appellation for God in this phrase, לַיהוָה צְבָאוֹת, effectively ends the first half of the oracle.

2:13 וְזֹאת שֵׁנִית תַּעֲשׂוּ כַּסּוֹת דִּמְעָה אֶת־מִזְבַּח יְהוָה בְּכִי וַאֲנָקָה מֵאֵין עוֹד פְּנוֹת אֶל־הַמִּנְחָה וְלָקַחַת רָצוֹן מִיֶּדְכֶם:

Verse 13 begins the second half of the oracle with a second complaint. The *waw* conjunction is conjunctive joining two similar situations, rather than disjunctive as indicated by the presence of the *pĕtûhâ* (פ) between verse 12 and 13 (see Hill, 236). Glazier-McDonald and others associate this verse with previous verses on mixed marriages (GM, 99–100). However, the verse seems to be the beginning of the pericope on divorce, with the consequence of priests' actions stated first and followed by the statement of the problem. This is a reversal of verses 10-12, thus forming a chiasm—A, B, B′, A′—accusation, consequence, consequence, accusation. The presence of this structure adds credibility to the *waw* conjunction at the beginning of the verse being conjunctive and not disjunctive.

וְזֹאת שֵׁנִית תַּעֲשׂוּ. *Waw* cop with demons pron f s + adj f s + Qal *yiqtol* 2 m pl √עָשָׂה. BHS proposes deleting this phrase (see BHS note 13ᵃ⁻ᵃ), but the use of שֵׁנִית to indicate a second issue or occurrence is common in prophetic literature. See Jer 1:13; 13:3; Ezek 4:6; Jonah 3:1; Hag 2:20; and Zech 4:12. וְזֹאת functions as a predicate adjective and is translated "and this is." The placement of the demonstrative pronoun and the adjective before the verb perhaps is for emphasis, stressing "second thing" (Niccacci, 85).

תַּעֲשׂוּ. The *yiqtol* is a progressive nonperfective, meaning that the action is continuous or on going (WO §31.3b).

כַּסּוֹת דִּמְעָה אֶת־מִזְבַּח יְהוָה בְּכִי וַאֲנָקָה. This is a subordinate clause, describing the consequence of the action of the subsequent clause.

כַּסּוֹת דִּמְעָה. Pi inf constr √כָּסָה + noun f coll (BDB, 199). The infinitive has a verbal characteristic, similar to that of a participial gerund. Hill suggests the infinitive construct here emphasizes the continuous action initiated by the nonperfective **תַּעֲשׂוּ** (Hill, 237). This is the first of a series of three infinitive construct phrases in this verse that have a verb/object sequence.

אֶת־מִזְבַּח יְהֹוָה. Sign of dir obj – noun m s constr + pr noun. The construct genitival phrase is the object of **כַּסּוֹת**.

בְּכִי וַאֲנָקָה. Noun m s + *waw* conj with noun f s. The phrase is an aside, describing the action that began in the previous phrase.

מֵאֵין עוֹד פְּנוֹת אֶל־הַמִּנְחָה. This is a negative infinitive clause of result.

מֵאֵין עוֹד. מִן prep with negative constr + adv. The combination of מִן and אֵין provide a causal negative for the infinitive, translated "so there is not" or "because there is not." The adverb takes on the sense of continuance (BDB, 728). The word does double duty and negates both of the following infinitives, **פְּנוֹת** and **לָקַחַת**. Gesenius points out that the double negative is emphatic, especially this combination (GKC §152*y*).

פְּנוֹת. Qal inf constr √פָּנָה. The verb literally means "turning toward" but is used figuratively here as "looking" or "regarding."

אֶל־הַמִּנְחָה. Prep – def art with noun f s. This is a datival phrase. The preposition אֶל can mean direction "to, toward" and have a specification of "concerning" (WO §11.2.2a).

וְלָקַחַת רָצוֹן מִיֶּדְכֶם:. This phrase is the second half of the clause and carries over the sense of **מֵאֵין עוֹד**. The *waw* conjunction following a negative has an alternative force, that is, it is a simple conjunction that joins phrases that list alternatives (WO §39.2.1b).

וְלָקַחַת רָצוֹן. *Waw* cop with Qal inf constr √לָקַח + noun m s. רָצוֹן is the direct object of **וְלָקַחַת**. **וְלָקַחַת** is synonymously paralleled to **פְּנוֹת** and רָצוֹן to **אֶל־הַמִּנְחָה** (Hill, 239–40). רָצוֹן is an accusative referring to the condition, attitude, or manner of acceptance of the offerings (Verhoef, 273).

מִיֶּדְכֶם. מִן prep with noun f s constr and 2 m pl pronominal suf. מִיֶּדְכֶם is the indirect object of וְלָקַחַת. The מִן preposition is locational, indicating the place of origin of the offering. The pronominal suffix refers to the priests and the noun is a collective singular. The word occurs five times in Malachi and always in the singular: 1:10, 13; 2:13; 3:2, 12. Hill points out that this prepositional phrase is an idiom for ownership (Hill, 240).

2:14 וַאֲמַרְתֶּם עַל־מֶה עַל כִּי־יְהוָה הֵעִיד בֵּינְךָ וּבֵין |
אֵשֶׁת נְעוּרֶיךָ אֲשֶׁר אַתָּה בָּגַדְתָּה בָּהּ וְהִיא חֲבֶרְתְּךָ
וְאֵשֶׁת בְּרִיתֶךָ:

Verse 14 begins the second half of the oracle. The scene turns to a rhetorical response by the audience, but spoken by the prophet. The question/answer prophetic disputation resumes and introduces the theme for this half of the oracle—divorce.

וַאֲמַרְתֶּם עַל־מֶה. Discourse with interrogative clause reporting the priests' questioning of the accusations in verse 13.

וַאֲמַרְתֶּם. *Waw* relative with Qal *qatal* 2 m pl √אָמַר. Discourse introducing the response of the priests. The *waw* functions in an adversative sense and is translated "but."

עַל־מֶה. Prep – interrog. This combination literally means "upon what" or "concerning what" but has the sense of "on what basis" or "why" (WO §18.3d).

עַל כִּי־יְהוָה הֵעִיד בֵּינְךָ וּבֵין אֵשֶׁת נְעוּרֶיךָ. The עַל כִּי preposition/conjunction combination introduces a causal clause (WO §38.4a). This clause introduces a prophetic litany against divorce.

יְהוָה. Pr noun. Subject of the clause, fronted before the verb for emphasis.

הֵעִיד. Hiph *qatal* 3 m s √עוּד. Hill calls this form a "persistent perfective," something that began in the past and continues into the present (Hill, 241; WO §30.5.1c). The term has legal connotations, especially in the prophetic dispute genre. This is also covenant language, which has legal connections (Stuart, 1337).

בֵּינְךָ וּבֵין | אֵשֶׁת נְעוּרֶיךָ. Prep with 2 m s pronominal suf + *waw* cop with prep + noun f s constr + noun m pl constr with 2 m s pronominal suf. The discourse has become more personal, with the writer using second person singular pronouns instead of plural ones. The preposition בֵּין used in pairs has an exclusive sense, occurring 24 times in priestly and legal texts (WO §11.2.6c). Here the prepositions separate persons. Hill notes the combination בֵּין . . . הֵעִיד וּבֵין is only found Gen 31:44, another covenant scene where Jacob and Laban make a covenant (Hill, 241). The phrase is remarkably similar to the curse pronounced upon the serpent in Gen 3:15, which reads בֵּינְךָ וּבֵין הָאִשָּׁה. The genitival phrase אֵשֶׁת נְעוּרֶיךָ probably means first wife (Hill, 241) and one the man is legally attached to in covenant (Verhoef, 274).

אֲשֶׁר אַתָּה בָּגַדְתָּה בָּהּ. Rel pron + indep pers pron 2 m s + Qal *qatal* 2 m s √בָּגַד + בְּ prep with 3 f s pronominal suf. This is a dependent relative clause directly accusing the priests of their faithlessness. Hill notes that this phrase is omitted from 4QXIIa (Hill, 241).

אַתָּה. The personal pronoun is the subject of the clause and is fronted before the verb for emphasis.

בָּגַדְתָּה. This is the same verb used in 2:10 and 11. The writer is using parallel thought between the priests' (and people's) actions toward Yahweh and toward their wives.

בָּהּ. The בְּ preposition often occurs with בָּגַד and indicates a circumstance of specification according to Hill and translated "with" (Hill, 242); however, the meaning of the verb "act treacherously" is an adversative action so the preposition seems best translated in a similar manner as "against."

וְהִיא חֲבֶרְתְּךָ וְאֵשֶׁת בְּרִיתֶךָ: Epexegetical dependent clause giving additional information concerning אֵשֶׁת נְעוּרֶיךָ. The double, paralleled expressions emphasize the closeness of the marriage relationship.

וְהִיא חֲבֶרְתְּךָ. *Waw* conj with indep pers pron 3 f s + noun f s constr with 2 m s pronominal suf. This is a verbless clause with הִיא functioning as the subject and חֲבֶרְתְּךָ as predicate. The *waw* is conjunctive. The attributes of הִיא are in apposition to אַתָּה. The noun חֲבֶרְתְּךָ is found only here in the Hebrew Bible. Hill says this word is one indicating "permanent bonding" (Hill, 242).

וְאֵשֶׁת בְּרִיתֶךָ: *Waw* cop with noun f s constr + noun f s constr with 2 m s pronominal suf. This genitival phrase is unique to this verse in the Hebrew Bible. בְּרִיתֶךָ is parallel to בְּרִית in 2:10 and probably is intended to connect the covenant of Yahweh with the covenant of marriage.

2:15 וְלֹא־אֶחָד עָשָׂה וּשְׁאָר רוּחַ לוֹ וּמָה הָאֶחָד מְבַקֵּשׁ
זֶרַע אֱלֹהִים וְנִשְׁמַרְתֶּם בְּרוּחֲכֶם וּבְאֵשֶׁת נְעוּרֶיךָ
אַל־יִבְגֹּד:

This is a difficult verse to translate because it lacks a few elements necessary for it to make sense, therefore, it leads to a variety of translations. For more details on its difficulty, see the discussion in Hill, 243–44. Stuart calls verse 15 a "cryptic puzzle" (Stuart, 1340). Furthermore, he says ". . . it simply does not read like normal Hebrew, and combines terms and concepts that are not otherwise found together in Scripture. In other words, it is not at all clear what point(s) three-fourths of verse 15 is making" (Stuart, 1341). *BHS* note 15[a–a] suggests that verse 15 is a later addition.

וְלֹא־אֶחָד עָשָׂה וּשְׁאָר רוּחַ לוֹ. This first clause seems to be missing a subject or an object and therefore is difficult to translate.

וְלֹא־אֶחָד. *Waw* conj with neg – noun m s. The *waw* is a coordinating conjunction with the negative. לֹא functions as an item negation rather than a clausal negation, which is rare in Biblical Hebrew (see WO §39.3.2a; GKC §152*e*). Furthermore, the coordinating *waw* and negative adverb construction are understood in many Bible translations as a negative interrogative (Hill, 244), thus essentially emending the text to read הֲלֹא. However, the interrogative is not present and is implied here only because the following clause is parallel to this one and it is a question. אֶחָד is a nonspecific cardinal numeral and is either the subject or object of עָשָׂה. Either way, אֶחָד is in an emphatic position. Whether subject or object, the one not represented by אֶחָד is necessary for understanding the clause but it is missing. Also, the translator must decide to whom אֶחָד is referring, which is not clear. Is it referring to Yahweh (as Niccacci, 65), the priest who married a foreign woman, the foreign woman, Adam, Abraham, or something else? (See GM, 103–5.) Hill makes a compelling argument that אֶחָד parallels its usage in 2:10, in which case it refers to Yahweh (Hill, 246; as does GM, 106). In the context of the verse, the clause can be read, "Did he not make [them] one?," referring to the oneness of marriage. However, this reading has its difficulties too. The LXX reads ἄλλος or "other" instead of "one." My preference is that אֶחָד is the subject and refers to those who married a foreign woman.

עָשָׂה. Qal *qatal* 3 m s √עָשׂה.

וּשְׁאָר רוּחַ לוֹ. *Waw* conj with noun m s constr + noun f s + לְ prep with 3 m s pronominal suf. The *waw* is conjunctive has an epexegetical sense, conjoining this phrase with the previous one and clarifying it. This genitival phrase שְׁאָר רוּחַ is unique in the Masoretic Text. רוּחַ refers to "life force" given by Yahweh. Here it includes the ability to procreate, as this phrase is in parallel with זֶרַע אֱלֹהִים in the next clause (GM, 108). The לְ preposition marks the indirect object and indicates possession (WO §11.2.10d). The third person masculine singular suffix marks the indirect object and refers back to the same person as אֶחָד. Stuart and others suggest that the suffix should be second person masculine singular (Stuart, 1341); however, there is no textual evidence for this emendation. Keil and Delitzsch argue that this clause is a subordinate clause and is descriptive of the subject of the previous clause, אֶחָד (KD, 652).

וּמָה֙ הָאֶחָ֔ד מְבַקֵּ֖שׁ זֶ֣רַע אֱלֹהִ֑ים. Interrogative clause closely connected to the previous clause as indicated by the coordinating *waw* conjunction and by the repetition of אֶחָד. Some translators (Smith, 319; Petersen, 194) treat this clause as one while others (Hill, 221; GM, 82; Stuart, 1338) treat זֶ֣רַע אֱלֹהִים as a second clause. Keil and Delitzsch identify מְבַקֵּשׁ זֶ֣רַע אֱלֹהִים as the second clause (KD, 651), with the first clause carrying over עָשָׂה as its predicate from the previous clause.

וּמָה֙ הָאֶחָ֔ד מְבַקֵּ֖שׁ. *Waw* conj with interrog + def art with noun m s + Pi ptc m s abs √בקשׁ. The cardinal numeral is definite here and refers to the previous usage of אֶחָד (see GKC §126c). The Piel participle indicates continuous or ongoing action.

זֶ֣רַע אֱלֹהִים. Noun m s constr + noun m pl. This phrase is the answer to the question of the previous clause. The noun אֱלֹהִים is being used in the superlative sense and shows that the "offspring" originated from and belong to Yahweh (WO §14.5b).

וְנִשְׁמַרְתֶּ֖ם בְּרוּחֲכֶ֑ם. A sequential clause of logical action. Note that the prophet changes back to the second person plural pronouns, indicating that he is again addressing a wider audience, as in 2:14a.

וְנִשְׁמַרְתֶּ֖ם. Niph *wᵉqatal* 2 m pl √שׁמר. The conjunction functions as a nonperfective sequential *waw*, like a *waw* consecutive, with a logical action to the previous clause (WO §32.2.3d). It expresses what the subject ought to do. The *wᵉqatal* verb form has a force near that of an imperative.

בְּרוּחֲכֶ֑ם. בְּ prep with noun f s constr and 2 m pl pronominal suf. The בְּ preposition has a spatial sense, thus translated as "in" (WO §11.2.5b). The second use of רוּחַ is a reminder of its first use, perhaps a word play (Hill, 248). This form is unique in the Masoretic Text to Mal 2:15 and 16.

וּבְאֵ֥שֶׁת נְעוּרֶ֖יךָ אַל־יִבְגֹּֽד׃. The *waw* is conjunctive, joining two related clauses with this one having the near imperative force of the previous one. This phrase echoes the wording in 2:14a and functions as an envelope to a literary subunit.

וּבְאֵשֶׁת נְעוּרֶיךָ‎. *Waw* conj with בְּ prep and noun f s constr +
noun m pl constr with 2 m s pronominal suf. This is the indirect
object. It is fronted, that is, it precedes the verb and is emphasized or
focused upon because of its position (MNK, 345–46). The בְּ preposition functions as an adversative and is translated "against" (WO
§11.2.5d).

אַל־יִבְגֹּד׃‎. Neg – Qal *yiqtol* 3 m s √בָּגַד‎. This is a third person
form but a few Hebrew manuscripts, LXX, Targums, and Vulgate
have a second person form (*BHS* note 15[d], GKC §144*p*). If the translator accepts the emendation, the negative + the second person *yiqtol* verb would form a negative imperative and reflect urgency (WO
§34.2.1b). However, Hill points out that the third singular form
makes sense here if the subject is understood to be an indefinite warn-
ing, not directed toward a specific person or group of persons (Hill,
249). Given the second person singular suffix on the indirect object
and the second person subject on the verb of the preceding clause, I
prefer emending the text to read with a second person singular subject.

2:16 כִּי־שָׂנֵא שַׁלַּח אָמַר יְהוָה אֱלֹהֵי יִשְׂרָאֵל וְכִסָּה חָמָס
עַל־לְבוּשׁוֹ אָמַר יְהוָה צְבָאוֹת וְנִשְׁמַרְתֶּם בְּרוּחֲכֶם
וְלֹא תִבְגֹּדוּ׃

Much like verse 15, verse 16 has difficulties. Translating the verse
depends upon how one translates the first word, as the adverb כִּי governs the sense of the entire verse.

כִּי־שָׂנֵא שַׁלַּח אָמַר יְהוָה אֱלֹהֵי יִשְׂרָאֵל‎. Purpose clause.

כִּי‎. The clausal adverb כִּי introduces a purpose clause, translated
"for" or "because." The LXX, Targums, and Vulgate translate כִּי as a
conditional conjunction "if" (Stuart, 1341–42). Hill translates כִּי as
emphatic "indeed," citing Waltke and O'Connor for support (Hill,
249; WO §39.3.4e).

שָׂנֵא‎. Qal *qatal* 3 m s √שָׂנֵא‎. The *qatal* third person singular form of the verb does not make sense with the following phrase declaring this phrase a direct quotation. Rather, a first person singular pronoun is expected/needed. *BHS* note 16[a] and many translators suggest emending the text to read the first common singular pronoun "I" although no known ancient text has this construction. Gesenius and Verhoef suggest the pointing of the text be emended to that of a participle with the first person pronoun suppressed (GKC §116*s*; Verhoef, 278; KD, 653). The participle would be translated as a continuous state in the present tense, "hates." However, this construction of a participle without the pronoun lacks the emphasis that an emphatic clause requires and is not consistent with similar statements in Malachi, such as 1:3 where the *qatal* first person common singular form is used or 2:9 where the pronoun אֲנִי is used. The Qumran text 4QXIIa has a second person form "you hate." Given the presence of the messenger formula following the phrase, the first person form is probably the intended translation. Hill suggests reading the Masoretic Text as it is, in the third person, and understands the subject to be Yahweh, who is הָאֶחָד of 2:15 (Hill, 250). For more information on שָׂנֵא, see note on this word in 1:3.

שַׁלַּח. Pi inf constr √שָׁלַח. The word means "to send away" but is usually translated "divorce" (see BDB, 1019). This word is usually translated as the object of שָׂנֵא. The word as pointed can be a Piel imperative since the Piel infinitive construct and imperative have the same form. However, a command to divorce seems out of place unless it is stated sarcastically.

אָמַר יְהוָה אֱלֹהֵי יִשְׂרָאֵל. Prophetic messenger formula as used previously in Malachi, but with the addition of the genitival phrase אֱלֹהֵי יִשְׂרָאֵל, descriptive of יְהוָה. *BHS* note 16[b–b] suggests that אֱלֹהֵי יִשְׂרָאֵל is a later addition. This phrase seems odd here when compared to other messenger formula statements in Malachi, as it only occurs here in the book.

וְכִסָּה חָמָס עַל־לְבוּשׁוֹ אָמַר יְהוָה צְבָאוֹת. This clause with the *waw* conjunction is interpreted as a parallel clause to the previous one (*waw* = and), as a consequential clause (*waw* = then), or as a causal clause (*waw* = for; Hill, 251). Whatever the case, the phrase is idiomatic of injustice done to one's wife. Moreover, the writer probably intended for the clause to parallel a similar clause in 2:13, כַּסּוֹת דִּמְעָה אֶת־מִזְבַּח יְהוָה, "covering with tears the altar of the Lord."

וְכִסָּה. Pi *wᵉqatal* 3 m s √כָּסָה. The verb כִּסָּה combined with the preposition עַל takes the meaning of "cover over" (GKC §119*bb*).

חָמָס. Noun m s. Indir obj of וְכִסָּה but may be the subject (as with LXX and Vulgate; see Verhoef, 279–80). Its location following the verb allows for either possibility. The noun חָמָס functioning as the indirect object makes better sense in this context because this places the married man as the source of the action (cf. Stuart, 1339).

עַל־לְבוּשׁוֹ. Prep – noun m s constr with 3 m s pronominal suf. Direct object of וְכִסָּה. The preposition עַל takes on the meaning of "over" when used after ideas of covering, translated "covering over" or "concealing" (GKC §119*bb*).

אָמַר יְהוָה צְבָאוֹת. Prophetic messenger formula.

וְנִשְׁמַרְתֶּם בְּרוּחֲכֶם וְלֹא תִבְגֹּדוּ׃. A sequential clause of logical action. This clause is almost identical to the one at the end of 2:15. The clause effectively ends the third oracle.

וְנִשְׁמַרְתֶּם. Niph *wᵉqatal* 2 m pl √שָׁמַר.

בְּרוּחֲכֶם. בְּ prep with noun f s constr and 2 m pl pronominal suf. See note on this word in 2:15.

וְלֹא תִבְגֹּדוּ׃. *Waw* cop with neg + Qal *yiqtol* 2 m pl √בָּגַד. The negative לֹא and the *yiqtol* second person plural verb form a negative command.

Fourth Oracle: God Sends Justice (2:17–3:5)

Malachi 2:17–3:5

2:17 "You have wearied Yahweh with your words. But you say, 'How have we wearied [him]?' When you say, 'Everyone doing evil is good in the eyes of Yahweh and in them he delights' or 'where is the God of justice?' 3:1 Behold, I am sending my messenger and he will clear a path before me. Then suddenly he will enter his temple, the Lord whom you are seeking and the messenger of the covenant which you desire. Behold, he is coming," says Yahweh of hosts.

2 "But who can endure the day when he comes? And who can stand when he appears? For he will be as a refiner's fire and as a launderer's soap. 3 Then he will sit a refiner and a purifier of silver and then he will purify the sons of Levi and he will refine them as gold and as silver. Then they will be ones bringing forth to Yahweh an offering in righteousness. 4 Then the offering of Judah and Jerusalem will be pleasing to Yahweh as in days of old and former years.

5 So I will draw near to you for judgment and I will be a swift witness against sorcerers and against adulterers, against ones swearing falsely, against oppressors of a laborer's wages, a widow, and an orphan, and who thrust aside a foreigner and they do not fear me," says the Lord of hosts.

The fourth oracle begins with Malachi's question and answer, pseudo-dialogue style of prophetic disputation but then transitions to a prophetic monologue with Yahweh speaking of a time when he will come to his temple and bring forth judgment. Like in previous oracles, the perspective is Yahweh speaking in first person. The grammar in this section includes much more synonymous parallelism than previously used in the book of Malachi. This section is full of translating difficulties, hence a few textual variants in the LXX and multiple renderings in the various English translations. Also, unlike previous oracles, this oracle is replete with participles.

Key Words				
בְּרִית	חָפֵץ	טוֹב	יָגַע	מַלְאָךְ
מִנְחָה	מִשְׁפָּט	רַע		

2:17 הוֹגַעְתֶּם יְהוָה בְּדִבְרֵיכֶם וַאֲמַרְתֶּם בַּמָּה הוֹגָעְנוּ בֶּאֱמָרְכֶם כָּל־עֹשֵׂה רָע טוֹב בְּעֵינֵי יְהוָה וּבָהֶם | הוּא חָפֵץ אוֹ אַיֵּה אֱלֹהֵי הַמִּשְׁפָּט:

הוֹגַעְתֶּם יְהוָה בְּדִבְרֵיכֶם. Hiph *qatal* 2 m pl √יָגַע + pr noun + בְּ prep with noun m pl constr and 2 m pl pronominal suf. This is a declarative statement of complaint.

הוֹגַעְתֶּם. The verb יָגַע in the Hiphil is transitive and is translated "weary" or "exhaust." In prophetic disputation, it has the sense of exasperate or provoke as in losing patience (*NIDOT*, 2:401). The word occurs only here in Malachi (2 times), but is a favorite in Deutero-Isaiah where it occurs ten times.

יְהוָה. Dir obj of הוֹגַעְתֶּם.

בְּדִבְרֵיכֶם. The בְּ preposition marks a circumstance of instrument (WO §11.2.5d).

וַאֲמַרְתֶּם בַּמָּה הוֹגָעְנוּ. Rhetorical response to the complaint of the previous clause.

וַאֲמַרְתֶּם. Qal *weqatal* 2 m pl √אָמַר. *Waw* is adversative and translated "but."

בַּמָּה הוֹגָעְנוּ. בְּ prep with def art and interog + Hiph *qatal* 1 c pl √יָגַע. בַּמָּה is best translated "in what way" or "how." The usage here is similar to that in 1:2, 6, 7; and 3:7. The verb is the same Hiphil stem as in the previous clause, altered for person agreement, and is

repeated, which intensifies the comparative nature of the two statements. Although the verb requires an object, as seen in the first clause,
the object is missing here, an instance of gapping. Based upon the
previous clause, the implied object is Yahweh (see Stuart, 1346). The
absence of the object places additional emphasis upon the verb and
stresses the point of objection. *BHS* note 17ᵃ, citing the LXX, Targums, and Vulgate, suggests adding a third person singular pronominal suffix to the verb for a object, but this addition is not necessary for
understanding the text.

בְּאֶמָרְכֶם כָּל־עֹשֵׂה רָע טוֹב בְּעֵינֵי יְהֹוָה. Clause of rebuttal.

בְּ .בְּאֶמָרְכֶם prep with Qal inf constr √אָמַר and 2 m pl pronominal suf. The combination of a בְּ preposition, Qal infinitive construct,
and pronominal suffix functions as a temporal perfective clause "when
you say" with the pronominal suffix functioning as the subject (WO
§36.2.2b; see Kelley, 182).

כָּל־עֹשֵׂה רָע. Noun m s constr – Qal act ptc m s abs √עשׂה +
noun m s. An encompassing genitival phrase. The phrase is a hyperbole, an exaggeration (Hill, 262). Waltke and O'Connor call the
phrase a "genitive of measure" (WO §9.5.3f). The participle עֹשֵׂה is
the predicate of the clause describing a continuous action. רָע has the
connotation of moral turpitude and is associated with sin and guilt
(*NIDOT*, 3:1155).

טוֹב בְּעֵינֵי יְהֹוָה. Adj m s + בְּ prep with noun f pl constr + pr
noun. In Biblical Hebrew, טוֹב and רָע are antonyms; they are polar
opposites. These are the same terms used in Genesis of the tree of
the knowledge of good and evil in the Garden of Eden (Gen 2:17),
functioning as a merismus indication knowledge humans were not
supposed to possess (*NIDOT*, 2:354). In Malachi, these terms function similarly to phrasing in Deuteronomy, where they refer to those
who keep or disobey the covenant. See Deut 4:25; 6:18; 9:18; 12:25,
28; 13:19; 17:2; and 31:29. Owens indicates that טוֹב can be either

an adjective or a Qal active participle (Owens, 937; BDB, 373). Its context and placement with רַע suggest that the form is an adjective. בְּעֵינֵי יְהוָה is an anthropomorphism. The בְּ preposition marks a circumstance (WO §11.2.5d).

וּבָהֶם הוּא חָפֵץ. *Waw* cop with בְּ prep and 3 m pl pronominal suf + indep pers pron 3 m s + Qal *qatal* 3 m s √חָפֵץ. The *waw* is a simple conjunction joining the two clauses. The word order, object/subject/verb suggests that the object is emphasized. The בְּ preposition of specification indicating the realm of the action (WO §11.2.5e). חָפֵץ only occurs in the Qal and indicates the direction of one's heart or passion (*NIDOT*, 2:232). Compare חָפֵץ here with the use of the adjective חָפֵץ in 1:10, noun form in 3:12, and a participial form in 3:1.

אוֹ אַיֵּה אֱלֹהֵי הַמִּשְׁפָּט: Coordinate interrogative clause stating a complaint parallel in thought with the previous clause.

אוֹ. Clausal coordinating conjunction joins this clause with the previous one. The writer uses this word only here and in 1:8 and in both cases it opens an interrogative clause.

אַיֵּה אֱלֹהֵי הַמִּשְׁפָּט: Adverbial interrog + noun m pl constr + def art with noun m s. אַיֵּה is not used with verbs, as exemplified here (WO §18.4c). The term is used 3 times in Malachi (1:6 [2x] and 2:17). אֱלֹהֵי הַמִּשְׁפָּט also occurs in Isaiah 30:18. The word מִשְׁפָּט occurs here for the first of three times in Malachi (2:17; 3:5, 22). The occurrences here and in 3:5 form a literary envelope for the fourth oracle. Schultz points out that מִשְׁפָּט has a range of meanings from the narrow act of deciding court cases to the broader category of enacting social justice (*NIDOT*, 4:216–17). Hill argues that the article attached to מִשְׁפָּט indicates the word should be understood as "the judgment" as in the eschaton (Hill, 264). However, the context suggests that judgment is not what is lacking but rather overall good legal order or justice. Therefore, "justice" is the preferred translation here.

3:1 הִנְנִי שֹׁלֵחַ מַלְאָכִי וּפִנָּה־דֶרֶךְ לְפָנָי וּפִתְאֹם יָבוֹא
אֶל־הֵיכָלוֹ הָאָדוֹן | אֲשֶׁר־אַתֶּם מְבַקְשִׁים וּמַלְאַךְ
הַבְּרִית אֲשֶׁר־אַתֶּם חֲפֵצִים הִנֵּה־בָא אָמַר יְהוָה
צְבָאוֹת:

Verse 3:1 begins a series of clauses where the writer moves from past tense in 2:17 to the present and immediate future. This verse is an exclamation, a pronouncement of intention in response to the question of the previous clause. Glazier-McDonald points out that this verse is pivotal for the book of Malachi. She says it points back to the prophecy of 1:11, answers the question in the present (2:17), and looks to the future (GM, 129). This verse is strikingly similar to Exod 23:20, where Yahweh sends an angel before the people of Israel. Note the similarities below:

Mal 3:1	הִנֵּה אָנֹכִי שֹׁלֵחַ מַלְאָךְ לְפָנֶיךָ
Exod 20:34	הִנְנִי שֹׁלֵחַ מַלְאָכִי וּפִנָּה־דֶרֶךְ לְפָנָי

Based upon this similarity and Malachi's heavy use of covenant language, Hill says "my messenger" in Malachi should be associated with the messenger of the covenant (Hill, 265).

הִנְנִי שֹׁלֵחַ מַלְאָכִי וּפִנָּה־דֶרֶךְ לְפָנָי. Independent, declarative clause reporting ending action.

הִנְנִי שֹׁלֵחַ. Demons part (interj) with 1 c s pronominal suf + Qal act ptc m s abs √שָׁלַח. Waltke and O'Connor say that הִנֵּה introduces an "exclamation of immediacy" and that הִנֵּה and a participle indicate vivid immediacy (WO §40.2.1b). Genesius adds that the event is not only immediate but also sure to happen (GKC §116p). Stuart disagrees and says it does not necessarily mean it is in the immediate future (Stuart, 1350); however, the context here suggests that it should be translated as immediate future. The sending of one from Yahweh is echoed again in 3:23.

מַלְאָכִי. Noun m s constr with 1 c s pronominal suf. מַלְאָכִי is the indirect object of this verbless clause. The word means "my messenger" but is also a play on the name in the book's superscription (1:1). See note on מַלְאָכִי in 1:1.

וּפִנָּה־דֶרֶךְ לְפָנָי. Pi *weqatal* 3 m s √פנה – noun m s + prep with 1 c s pronominal suf. The *waw* is conjunctive carrying over the immediate future tense from the previous phrase into this one. The phrase is reminiscent of Isa 40:3 "prepare the way of Yahweh"; however, Isaiah uses the phrase indicating a second exodus, which is not the case here. לְפָנָי is a לְ preposition with the noun construct plural פְּנֵי. It literally means "to the face of me," an idiom meaning "before." Hill, citing Gesenius, argues that the word is not a compound preposition (Hill, 267; GKC §119c); however, the word occurs so often in Biblical Hebrew with this meaning that it can be treated simply as a single entity, as a preposition.

וּפִתְאֹם יָבוֹא אֶל־הֵיכָלוֹ. *Waw* conj with adv + Qal *yiqtol* 3 m s √בוא + prep – noun m s constr with 3 m s pronominal suf. The *waw* is disjunctive, marking the beginning of the next action and best translated "then" to indicate sequential action. פִּתְאֹם is an adverb occurring rarely in Biblical Hebrew and refers to a quick coming of an unexpected action (see BDB, 837). In prophetic literature, "suddenly" often refers to God's action (Isa 29:5; 30:13; Jer 6:26).

יָבוֹא. The *yiqtol* form is an incipient present nonperfective, meaning that the action begins at the time the words are spoken and continues into the future (see WO §31.3d). בוא followed by the preposition אֶל means "come into" or "enter."

הָאָדוֹן אֲשֶׁר־אַתֶּם מְבַקְשִׁים וּמַלְאַךְ הַבְּרִית אֲשֶׁר־אַתֶּם חֲפֵצִים. This phrase names the subject of the previous clause, הָאָדוֹן, and is descriptive of the subject. The clause contains two synonymously paralleled phrases joined by a *waw* conjunction.

הָאָדוֹן. Def art with noun m s. Subject of יָבוֹא and, at the same time, the direct object of מְבַקְשִׁים.

אֲשֶׁר־אַתֶּם מְבַקְשִׁים. Rel pron – indep pers pron 2 m pl + Pi ptc m pl abs √בָּקַשׁ. Dependent relative clause modifying הָאָדוֹן. The relative pronoun אֲשֶׁר has an accusative function (WO §19.3a). The second person plural pronoun is the subject of the clause and echoes the pseudo-dialogue found in much of Malachi. The pronoun refers to the same persons who are the subject of rhetorical questions of 2:17. The participle is the predicate of the clause.

וּמַלְאַךְ הַבְּרִית. *Waw* conj + noun m s constr + def art with noun f s. Genitival phrase synonymously paralleled with הָאָדוֹן. The *waw* functions epexegetically, paralleling הָאָדוֹן with מַלְאַךְ and referring to the same person. הַבְּרִית is a theme in the third oracle and the use of the word here connects the action of the messenger with the disputes of the previous oracles. הַבְּרִית, made definite by the article, refers to the covenant of Yahweh and not the marriage covenant. מַלְאַךְ הַבְּרִית is an unusual phrase and has no parallel in the Hebrew Bible.

אֲשֶׁר־אַתֶּם חֲפֵצִים. Rel pron – indep pers pron 2 m pl + Qal act ptc m s abs √חָפֵץ. This dependent relative clause synonymously parallels the dependent relative clause above and is grammatically identical. The participle חֲפֵצִים functions adjectivally and serves as the predicate of the clause. In an ironic twist, חֲפֵצִים used here describes someone for whom the people are longing. However, a form of the same term is used in 2:17 in the people's accusation that Yahweh "delights" in evildoers.

הִנֵּה־בָא אָמַר יְהוָה צְבָאוֹת: . Independent, declarative clause reporting pending action.

הִנֵּה־בָא. Demons part – Qal act ptc m s abs √בּוֹא. Owens suggests the form can be a Qal *qatal* 3 m s but the context of immediate future action combined with the writer's prolific use of participles in this verse suggests that בָא is a participle (cf. Owens, 937). Furthermore, הִנֵּה and a participle begin this verse; thus, ending the verse with the same grammatical structure gives a literary enveloping affect. The demonstrative particle is an exclamation of immediacy, as noted with the הִנֵּה clause at the beginning of this verse. The implied subject of this clause is "the messenger of the covenant" of the previous clause.

אָמַר יְהוָה צְבָאוֹת:. Prophetic messenger formula, concluding the thought and ending the paragraph. *BHS* note 1ᵃ⁻ᵃ suggests this phrase was added; however, there is no textual witness to warrant excising it from the Masoretic Text. It identifies the authority behind the declaration, is nonintrusive within its context, and should be retained.

3:2　　וּמִי מְכַלְכֵּל אֶת־יוֹם בּוֹאוֹ וּמִי הָעֹמֵד בְּהֵרָאוֹתוֹ כִּי־
הוּא כְּאֵשׁ מְצָרֵף וּכְבֹרִית מְכַבְּסִים:

Verse 2 has two sections. The first one is two clauses containing rhetorical questions. The second one, the latter clauses of the verse, gives reasoning for the implied answers of the rhetorical questions.

וּמִי מְכַלְכֵּל אֶת־יוֹם בּוֹאוֹ. Interrogative clause with a rhetorical question, requiring a negative answer. This clause is synonymously paralleled to the subsequent clause, each one having the order of conjunction with interrogative/participle/object. The parallel questions suggest urgency and immediacy.

וּמִי. *Waw* conj with interrog. The interclausal *waw* is disjunctive and introduces a clause that is in contrast to verse 3:1 (WO §39.2.3b). The interrogative has a nominative function.

מְכַלְכֵּל. Pilpel ptc m s abs √כּוּל. This middle vowel verb has the meaning of "enduring" (BDB, 465; *HALOT*, 463). This is an infrequent verb in Biblical Hebrew and the word occurs only here in Malachi.

אֶת־יוֹם בּוֹאוֹ. Sign of dir obj – noun m s constr + Qal inf constr √בּוֹא with 3 m s pronominal suf. The Qal infinitive completes the genitival phrase as a direct object of מְכַלְכֵּל and functions as an adverbial accusative (WO §36.2.1d). The third person singular pronominal suffix is a genitive showing possession, thus "his coming." The pronominal suffix is a substitute for the מַלְאַךְ of verse 1.

וּמִי הָעֹמֵד בְּהֵרָאוֹתוֹ. Interrogative clause with a rhetorical question (requiring a negative answer) and synonymously paralleled to the previous clause. Hill points out that this phrase alludes to "the day of Yahweh," which is a common theme in prophetic literature (Hill, 272) and is alluded to in the sixth oracle.

וּמִי. *Waw* cop with interrog. The *waw* is conjunctive, connecting this clause with the previous one.

הָעֹמֵד. Def art with Qal act ptc m s abs √עָמַד. עָמַד means "stand," with the sense of endurance (*NIDOT*, 3:432–33), as in "remain standing." The term parallels מְכַלְכֵּל of the previous clause.

בְּהֵרָאוֹתוֹ. בְּ prep with Niph inf constr √רָאָה and 3 m s pronominal suf. The בְּ preposition has a temporal sense of "when" (Kelley, 182). The pronominal suffix has a genitival function of possession. The infinitive construct functions as an adverbial accusative, just as the infinitive in the preceding clause.

כִּי־הוּא כְּאֵשׁ מְצָרֵף. This verbless clause is the first of two that form the second section of this verse.

כִּי־הוּא. Conj – indep pers pron 3 m s. כִּי is a subordinate conjunction introducing a logical noun clause (WO §39.3.4e). הוּא is a pronominal substitute for מַלְאַךְ of verse 1. The LXX adds εἰσπορεύεται, Greek for בּוֹא which means, "goes in." The text makes sense without the emendation; the future tense of the English "to be" is implied here.

כְּאֵשׁ מְצָרֵף. כְּ prep with noun f s constr + Pi ptc m s abs √צָרַף. The כְּ preposition is a comparison of agreement in manner or norm (WO §11.2.9b). The participle functions as an indefinite noun in this simile.

וּכְבֹרִית מְכַבְּסִים:. *Waw* cop with כְּ prep and noun f s constr + Pi ptc m pl abs √כָּבַס. This genitival phrase is a simile synonymously paralleled in thought and grammar with the previous clause. The *waw* is conjunctive, connecting this phrase with the previous one. The noun בֹּרִית is a rarely used word in the Hebrew Bible (used only here and in Jer 2:22; BDB, 141). The word בֹּרִית means "alkali" or "soap." The writer's choice of the word is perhaps wordplay on בְּרִית "covenant" in verse 1 (Stuart, 1353; GM, 148). The participle מְכַבְּסִים functions as a noun here also, just as in the previous phrase.

3:3 וְיָשַׁב מְצָרֵף וּמְטַהֵר כֶּסֶף וְטִהַר אֶת־בְּנֵי־לֵוִי וְזִקַּק אֹתָם כַּזָּהָב וְכַכָּסֶף וְהָיוּ לַיהוָה מַגִּישֵׁי מִנְחָה בִּצְדָקָה:

Verse 3 expounds upon the similes in the latter half of verse 2, further defining the imagery and the role of the messenger. *BHS* note 3/4[a] suggests verse 3 and 4 are later additions; however, they are necessary for congruency and they do not interrupt the flow of thought.

וְיָשַׁב מְצָרֵף וּמְטַהֵר כֶּסֶף. Relative clause of sequence.

וְיָשַׁב מְצָרֵף. Qal *wᵉqatal* 3 m s √יָשַׁב + Pi ptc m s abs √צָרַף. A *waw* relative + *qatal* verb in a relative clause indicate a consecutive or logical sequence, in which the *waw* is translated "then" (WO §32.1.1). Keil and Delitzsch and Verhoef argue that a smith "sits" at his work as a refiner, thus יָשַׁב should be translated as "sit" (KD, 657; Verhoef, 290–91) since Yahweh is in the act of working. However, Hill translates the term "remain," suggesting the idea of continuance (Hill, 274–75). The context suggests the nuance of the messenger taking his place in preparation for work rather than continuing it, thus "sit" is the better translation. מְצָרֵף functions as a noun and serves as the predicate of וְיָשַׁב.

וּמְטַהֵר כֶּסֶף. *Waw* cop with Pi ptc m s constr √טָהֵר + noun m s. The *waw* is a simple conjunction. The construct participle functions as a genitival noun in a construct chain. מְטַהֵר in this form is found only here and Lev 14:11 in the Hebrew Bible (BDB, 372).

וְטִהַר אֶת־בְּנֵי־לֵוִי. Pi *wᵉqatal* 3 m s √טָהֵר + sign of dir obj – noun m pl constr – pr noun. The *waw* relative + *wᵉqatal* function as a relative clause and indicate a consecutive or logical sequence, with the *waw* translated "then." בְּנֵי־לֵוִי is the object of טִהַר and refers to the priesthood.

וְזִקַּק אֹתָם כַּזָּהָב וְכַכָּסֶף. This clause is synonymously paralleled with the previous one in thought and grammar.

וְזִקַּק. Pi *wᵉqatal* 3 m s √זָקַק. The *waw* conjunction connects two parallel clauses. זָקַק occurs rarely in the Hebrew Bible (only 7 times), only here in the Piel form, and only here in Malachi (BDB, 279). וְזִקַּק parallels וְטִהַר of the previous clause.

אֹתָם. Sign of dir obj with 3 m pl pronominal suf. The pronoun is the object of וְזִקַּק and refers to "the sons of Levi."

כַּזָּהָב וְכַכָּסֶף. כְּ prep with def art and noun m s + *waw* cop with כְּ prep, def art, and noun m s. The כְּ preposition marks a comparison of agreement of manner or norm (WO §11.2.9b). זָהָב and כֶּסֶף are a common word pair, occurring 95 times in the Hebrew Bible (*NIDOT*, 2:683). The presence of the definite article here is unusual, but may be one of generic use identifying a class of materials rather than a singular quantity (WO §13.5.1f).

וְהָיוּ לַיהוָה מַגִּישֵׁי מִנְחָה בִּצְדָקָה: This clause continues the grammatical parallelism of the previous clauses.

וְהָיוּ. Qal *wᵉqatal* 3 c pl √הָיָה. The *waw* relative and *wᵉqatal* verb function the same as in the previous clauses.

לַיהוָה. Indir obj of וְהָיוּ. The לְ preposition signifies an indirect object of goal or purpose (WO §11.2.10d). It indicates ownership or possession.

מַגִּישֵׁי מִנְחָה בִּצְדָקָה: Hi ptc m pl constr √נָגַשׁ + noun f s + בְּ prep with noun f s. The phrase functions epexegetically, in apposition with the subject "sons of Levi" (Hill, 277). The participle functions as a construct genitive. The בְּ preposition is of circumstantial usage and marks a phrase that qualifies the realm of the action of the verb (WO §11.2.5e), in this case, the participle phrase מַגִּישֵׁי מִנְחָה.

מִנְחָה is a nonspecific term and includes various types of offerings such as animals, grains, vegetables, incense, and gifts (*NIDOT*, 2:980, 982, 985). Here, the emphasis is on the condition of the priest and not the offering.

3:4   וְעָרְבָה לַיהֹוָה מִנְחַת יְהוּדָה וִירוּשָׁלָ֑͏ִם כִּימֵי עוֹלָ֑ם
וּכְשָׁנִים קַדְמֹנִיּֽוֹת׃

Verse 4 continues the thought of verse 3. It begins with a *waw* relative + *qatal* verb, continuing and completing the grammatically similar series from verse 3.

וְעָרְבָה לַיהֹוָה מִנְחַת יְהוּדָה וִירוּשָׁלָ֑͏ִם. Relative clause of sequence.

וְעָרְבָה. Qal *weqatal* 3 f s √עָרֵב. The *waw* relative completes a logical series and should be translated "then." וְעָרְבָה is a stative verb.

לַיהֹוָה. לְ prep with pr noun. Indir obj of וְעָרְבָה. The לְ preposition marks an indirect object of goal (WO §11.2.10d).

מִנְחַת יְהוּדָה וִירוּשָׁלָ֑͏ִם. Noun f s constr + pr noun + *waw* cop with pr noun. This construct genitival phrase is the subject of וְעָרְבָה. According to Hill, the mentioning of the state and the capital city is inclusive and represents the entire covenant community (Hill, 279).

כִּימֵי עוֹלָ֑ם וּכְשָׁנִים קַדְמֹנִיּֽוֹת׃. These phrases refer to a past time when Israel was faithful to Yahweh.

כִּימֵי עוֹלָ֑ם. כְּ prep with noun m pl constr + noun m s. This genitival phrase is an idiom of ancient days, or as Glazier-McDonald says, "the good old days" (GM, 155). The כְּ preposition is a comparative, an agreement in a manner or norm (WO §11.2.9b).

וּכְשָׁנִים קַדְמֹנִיּֽוֹת׃. *Waw* cop with כְּ prep and noun f pl + adj f pl. The כְּ preposition functions as the one in the phrase above. The adjective is attributive, modifying the plural noun.

וְקָרַבְתִּי אֲלֵיכֶם לַמִּשְׁפָּט וְהָיִיתִי | עֵד מְמַהֵר 3:5
בַּמְכַשְּׁפִים וּבַמְנָאֲפִים וּבַנִּשְׁבָּעִים לַשָּׁקֶר וּבְעֹשְׁקֵי
שְׂכַר־שָׂכִיר אַלְמָנָה וְיָתוֹם וּמַטֵּי־גֵר וְלֹא יְרֵאוּנִי
אָמַר יְהוָה צְבָאוֹת:

In verse 5, Yahweh answers the question raised in 2:17, "Where is the God of justice?" Hill points out that the word מִשְׁפָּט frames the oracle (Hill, 279).

וְקָרַבְתִּי אֲלֵיכֶם לַמִּשְׁפָּט. Clause of consequence.

וְקָרַבְתִּי אֲלֵיכֶם. Qal *weqatal* 1 c s √קָרַב + prep with 2 m pl pronominal suf. Hill defines the *waw* conjunction as an emphatic *waw* (Hill, 279; WO §39.2.1b), however, the *waw* may be consequential and translated "so" or "then." The *waw* relative + *qatal* form continues the nonperfective (future tense) sense established in the preceding verses. Glazier-McDonald points out that אֶל + קָרַב means "draw near" or "approach." אֲלֵיכֶם is the direct object of וְקָרַבְתִּי. The preposition אֶל marks the direction of movement (WO §11.2.2a). The phrase corresponds to and is synonymous with בּוֹא in 3:1 (GM, 155–56).

לַמִּשְׁפָּט. לְ prep with def art and noun m s. Indir obj of וְקָרַבְתִּי. The לְ preposition indicates an indirect object of purpose (WO §11.2.10d). מִשְׁפָּט means more than "judgment" as in deciding a court case, but also includes "justice" as in setting right any injustice. See *CHAL*, 221; *NIDOT*, 2:1144. Hill notes that the noun is definite and may refer to a specific judgment, the eschaton, as in 2:17 above (Hill, 280).

וְהָיִיתִי עֵד מְמַהֵר בַּמְכַשְּׁפִים וּבַמְנָאֲפִים וּבַנִּשְׁבָּעִים לַשָּׁקֶר וּבְעֹשְׁקֵי שְׂכַר־שָׂכִיר אַלְמָנָה וְיָתוֹם וּמַטֵּי־גֵר. The thought of the previous clause in the nonperfective future sense continues in this clause, as it defines the object of Yahweh's judgment. The clause contains a string of participles functioning as substantives.

וְהָיִיתִי עֵד מְמַהֵר. Qal *wᵉqatal* 1 c s √הָיָה + noun m s + Pi ptc m s abs √מָהַר. The *waw* relative continues the nonperfective future tense of the preceding clause. עֵד is the predicate nominative of וְהָיִיתִי. The Piel participle functions as an attributive adjective, modifying עֵד.

בַּמְכַשְּׁפִים וּבַמְנָאֲפִים. בְּ prep with def art and Pi ptc m pl abs √כָּשַׁף + *waw* cop with בְּ prep and def art and Pi ptc m pl abs √נָאַף. Both participles function as substantives. The בְּ prepositions are adversative, thus translated "against" (WO §11.2.5d).

וּבַנִּשְׁבָּעִים לַשָּׁקֶר. *Waw* cop with בְּ prep and def art and Niph ptc m pl abs √שָׁבַע + לְ prep with def art and noun m s. The *waw*, בְּ preposition, and participle function the same way here as they do in the previous phrase. לַשָּׁקֶר modifies וּבַנִּשְׁבָּעִים. The לְ preposition has a sense of manner (WO §11.2.10d) with לַשָּׁקֶר translated adverbially. According to *BHS* note 5ᵃ, multiple Hebrew manuscripts and the LXX add "by my name" to this phrase, perhaps due to a similar reading in Zech 5:4.

וּבְעֹשְׁקֵי שְׂכַר־שָׂכִיר. *Waw* cop with בְּ prep and Qal act ptc m s constr √עָשַׁק + noun m s – adj m s. This is the same grammatical construction as above. שְׂכַר־שָׂכִיר is a construct genitive phrase translated "wages of the laborer." *BHS* note 5ᵇ suggests this is dittography and recommends deleting the second word; however, the phrase makes better sense as it stands.

אַלְמָנָה וְיָתוֹם וּמַטֵּי־גֵר. Noun f s + *waw* cop with noun m s + *waw* cop with Hiph ptc m pl constr √נָטָה – noun m s. This phrase continues the list of objects of וּבְעֹשְׁקֵי in the previous phrase. As Hill points out, אַלְמָנָה and יָתוֹם are often paired (even with גֵר) in contexts where social justice is an issue (Hill, 282; Deut 24:20; Jer 22:3; Ezek 22:7; Zech 7:10; etc.). גֵר is a foreigner who dwells in the land (*TDOT*, 2:443, 447). *BHS* note 5ᶜ⁻ᶜ suggests placing וּמַטֵּי־גֵר before אַלְמָנָה and adding the adversative בְּ preposition. Although the Hebrew text would read more smoothly with this emendation, no ancient texts support this change.

וְלֹא יְרֵא֫וּנִי אָמַר יְהוָה צְבָא֑וֹת: . This clause is a summation of those listed in the previous clause.

וְלֹא יְרֵא֫וּנִי. *Waw* cop and neg + Qal *qatal* 3 c pl √יָרֵא with 1 c s pronominal suf. The epexegetical *waw* joins this clause with the previous one. Since this clause summarizes the previous one, the *waw* can be translated "that is" (see Hill, 259; WO §39.2.4a). יְרֵא֫וּנִי is a stative verb indicating an emotional response, in this case to Yahweh (WO §30.5.3). The pronominal suffix, the object of the verb, refers to Yahweh.

אָמַר יְהוָה צְבָא֑וֹת: . Prophetic messenger formula, effectively concluding the fourth oracle.

Fifth Oracle: Community Called
to Support the Cult (3:6-12)

Malachi 3:6-12

⁶"Indeed, I, Yahweh, I do not change, therefore, you, children of Jacob have not ceased. ⁷From the days of your ancestors you turned from my statutes and you have not kept [them]. Return to me so that I might return to you," says Yahweh of hosts. "But you say, 'How do we return?' ⁸Will a person rob God? For you are robbing me. But you say, 'How have we robbed you?' The tithe and the offering! ⁹With the curse you are being cursed, indeed, it is me you are robbing—the entire nation! ¹⁰Bring all the tithe into the storehouse so that food will be in my house. Test me in this," says Yahweh of hosts, "See if I will not open the windows of heaven and I will pour out to you a blessing that is beyond sufficiency. ¹¹And I will rebuke for you the devourer and it will not ruin the fruit of the ground for you and the vine of the field will not fail to bear for you," says Yahweh of hosts. ¹²"Then all nations will call you blessed for you, you will be a land of delight," says Yahweh of hosts.

The fifth oracle is closely related to and continues the thought of the fourth oracle. The Masoretic Text does not divide the fourth and fifth oracles, instead placing the *petûḥâ sĕtûmâ* (the *sāmek* denoting separation of literary units) before 2:14 and after 3:12 (see Hill, 291–92, and MNK, 48 for a discussion of this feature). The fifth oracle continues in the prophetic disputation style, including the pseudo-dialogue of questions and answers. According to Wendland, the entire unit is a chiasm (Wendland, 118):

A Introduction, divine premise (6)

   B Appeal, repent (7)

C Indictment, "you have robbed me" (8)

    D Verdict, curse (9a)

C′ Indictment, "you are robbing me" (9b)

 B′ Promise, blessings (10-11)

A′ Conclusion, Messianic vision (12)

Key Words				
אָרַר	בָּחַן	בְּרָכָה	גּוֹי	מַעֲשֵׂר
קָבַע	שׁוּב	שָׂכַל	שָׁנָה	תְּרוּמָה

3:6   כִּי אֲנִי יְהוָה לֹא שָׁנִיתִי וְאַתֶּם בְּנֵי־יַעֲקֹב לֹא כְלִיתֶם:

The verse contains two phrases having identical construction: personal pronoun/proper name/negative/verb. Both are emphasizing the subject of the phrase.

כִּי אֲנִי יְהוָה לֹא שָׁנִיתִי. Conj + indep pers pron 1 c s + pr noun + neg + Qal *qatal* 1 c s √שָׁנָה. כִּי functions as either a coordinating conjunction meaning "for" or "because" (as GM, 173), or as an emphatic adverb "indeed" or "truly" (Verhoef, 299). Stuart treats it as a coordinating conjunction "since" (Stuart, 1360). If one translates כִּי as a coordinating conjunction, then the clause is a subordinate clause, dependent upon verse 5 for meaning. However, if כִּי is translated as an emphatic adverb, then the clause is an independent clause. The combination of the first common singular pronoun coupled with proper noun may be translated as a self-introduction formula, "I am Yahweh" or as an appositional construction "I, Yahweh" which is emphatic. If the second translation is correct, then this lends credibility to כִּי also being translated as an emphatic adverb.

לֹא שָׁנִיתִי. The *qatal* first common singular verb שָׁנִיתִי, coupled with the negative, can be translated as a continuous perfective, meaning both "I have not changed" and "I do not change." The verb שָׁנָה has Yahweh as the subject three times in the Masoretic Text (Job

14:20; Ps 89:35; and Mal 3:6). In Malachi, the term refers to Yahweh's
faithfulness to the covenant (*NIDOT*, 4: 191).

וְאַתֶּם בְּנֵי־יַעֲקֹב לֹא כְלִיתֶם׃. *Waw* conj with indep pers
pron 2 m pl + noun m pl constr – pr noun + negative + Qal *qatal* 2
m pl √כָּלָה. The *waw* is disjunctive, marking the contrast between
Yahweh and Jacob. The personal pronoun אַתֶּם is in contrast to אֲנִי
of the previous phrase. Likewise, בְּנֵי־יַעֲקֹב is in contrast to יְהוָה.
Hill points out that the genitival phrase בְּנֵי־יַעֲקֹב can be translated
as vocative, "O descendents of Jacob" which is in keeping with the
emphatic nature of the verse (Hill, 296–97). The *qatal* verb כְלִיתֶם
means "bring to an end" or "destroy" (BDB, 477). The implication
here is that neither Yahweh nor the descendents of Jacob have changed
their ways. The phrase only makes sense if the translator considers
the meaning of the word יַעֲקֹב—"supplanter" (BDB, 784)—in this
context.

לְמִימֵי אֲבֹתֵיכֶם סַרְתֶּם מֵחֻקַּי וְלֹא שְׁמַרְתֶּם שׁוּבוּ   3:7
אֵלַי וְאָשׁוּבָה אֲלֵיכֶם אָמַר יְהוָה צְבָאוֹת וַאֲמַרְתֶּם
בַּמֶּה נָשׁוּב׃

The prophet again uses direct commands and pseudo-dialogue in a
question and answer format to deliver his message.

לְמִימֵי אֲבֹתֵיכֶם סַרְתֶּם מֵחֻקַּי וְלֹא שְׁמַרְתֶּם. Independent,
declarative clause.

לְמִימֵי אֲבֹתֵיכֶם. לְ prep with מִן prep and noun m pl constr +
noun m pl constr with 2 m pl pronominal suf. The preposition combination is found in the Hebrew Bible only here and in 2 Kgs 19:25. The
לְ preposition is a temporal *lamed* indicating a location in time (WO
§11.2.10c) while the מִן preposition indicates a beginning point in
time (WO §11.2.11c). This combination of prepositions marks time
that began at a point in the past (the days of your fathers) and continues into the present.

סַרְתֶּם. Qal *qatal* 2 m p √סוּר. The verb סוּר has the meaning of turning aside, as turning away from one's intended path (BDB, 693). The perfective verb indicates completed action in past time.

מֵחֻקַּי. Prep with noun m pl constr and 1 c s pronominal suf. The מִן preposition in the ablative sense indicates movement away (WO §11.2.11c), in this case, away from "my statutes."

וְלֹא שְׁמַרְתֶּם. *Waw* cop with neg + Qal *qatal* 2 m pl √שָׁמַר. The *waw* copulative is a simple coordinating conjunction. The object of the phrase is implied and understood as "them" (Stuart, 1364).

שׁוּבוּ אֵלַי וְאָשׁוּבָה אֲלֵיכֶם אָמַר יְהוָה צְבָאוֹת. The clause has parallel construction, two phrases consisting of verb אֶל preposition/pronominal suffix. The disjunctive *waw* indicates that the second phrase is conditional upon proper action by those addressed in the first phrase (Hill, 302).

שׁוּבוּ אֵלַי. Qal impv 2 m pl √שׁוּב + prep with 1 c s pronominal suf. A cohortative following another volitional form (in this case an imperative) usually gives a sense of purpose to a clause and is translated "so that" or "in order that." The imperative gives urgency to the request, requiring an immediate and specific answer (WO §34.4a). שׁוּב is a commonly used term in covenantal passages (see GM, 184–85), especially in the imperative form in prophetic literature. It has the connotation of repentance for people who have had moral or spiritual lapses (*NIDOT*, 4:56–57). The preposition אֵלַי indicates a direction "toward" (WO §11.2.2a), in this case, the opposite movement of the מִן preposition of the previous clause.

וְאָשׁוּבָה אֲלֵיכֶם. Qal *wᵉyiqtol* 1 c s √שׁוּב + prep with 2 m pl pronominal suf. This is a dependent clause, connected to the previous clause. It indicates a purpose or result (Hill, 302). The *waw* is disjunctive and shifts the scene to another participant (Hill, 302; WO §39.2.3c). It is conditional upon the action by the participants of the first phrase should the translated "so that." וְאָשׁוּבָה is a cohortative form and indicates a desired outcome. אֶל is a directional preposition, translated "to." The pronouns in this and the previous phrase create an A/B//B′/A′ construction (you, me, I, you). The second person pro-nominal suffix is the indirect object of וְאָשׁוּבָה.

אָמַר יְהֹוָה צְבָאֽוֹת. Prophetic messenger formula.

וַאֲמַרְתֶּם בַּמֶּה נָשֽׁוּב׃. Qal *weqatal* 2 m pl √אָמַר + ב prep with interrog + Qal *yiqtol* 1 c pl √שׁוּב. For information on וַאֲמַרְתֶּם, see note in 1:2. בַּמֶּה, the preposition/interrogative combination, is best translated "in what way" or "how." See note on the same word in 2:17. For information on the meaning of נָשׁוּב, see note on שֽׁוּבוּ above.

3:8 הֲיִקְבַּע אָדָם אֱלֹהִים כִּי אַתֶּם קֹבְעִים אֹתִי וַאֲמַרְתֶּם בַּמֶּה קְבַעֲנֽוּךָ הַֽמַּעֲשֵׂר וְהַתְּרוּמָֽה׃

הֲיִקְבַּע אָדָם אֱלֹהִים כִּי אַתֶּם קֹבְעִים אֹתִי. Interrogative clause joined to an emphatic clause.

הֲיִקְבַּע אָדָם אֱלֹהִים. Interrog with Qal *yiqtol* 3 m s √קָבַע + noun m s + noun m pl. The interrogative marks a rhetorical question with an obvious answer, a common construction in Malachi. Waltke and O'Connor call this *yiqtol* verb form a nonperfective of desire (WO §31.4h). Both אָדָם and אֱלֹהִים are generic terms. קָבַע is a rare verb, occurring only in Mal 2:8 [3x], 9; and Prov 22:23. KB suggest the word means "betray" rather than "rob" in this verse (*HALOT*, 1062). The context allows for the richness of both meanings, where Yahweh is being "betrayed" and "robbed." אָדָם is a collective sin-gular and should be translated "a person" or "anyone." Also, אֱלֹהִים is generic of יְהֹוָה, the name of God so commonly used in Malachi. This generic phrase sets up the following specific and confrontational phrase. Note that *BHS*, following LXX, suggests amending הֲיִקְבַּע to הֲיַעֲקֹב, making the verb a wordplay on the name "Jacob," but this emendation is not necessary for understanding the text (*BHS*, note 8ᵃ). Likewise, the LXX emends the other occurrence of קָבַע in this verse similarly.

כִּי אַתֶּם קֹבְעִים אֹתִי. Conj + indep pers pron 2 m pl + Qal ptc

m pl abs √קָבַע + sign of dir obj with 1 c s pronominal suf. כִּי functions as a coordinating conjunction, translated "because" or "for" and
introduces an emphatic clause (Hill, 304). The participle functions
as the verb of this clause indicating continuous action in present time
(WO §37.6b). The pronoun אַתֶּם serves as the subject of the clause.
The pronoun's position before the verb makes it emphatic, especially
so since the previous phrase, the one this phase is paralleling, has the
verb/subject in normal Biblical Hebrew order. This phrase is more
specific and more intense than the previous one, replacing the generic
terms אָדָם with אַתֶּם and אֱלֹהִים with אֹתִי.

וַאֲמַרְתֶּם בַּמֶּה קְבַעֲנוּךָ. Qal *weqatal* 2 m pl √אָמַר + בְּ prep with
interrog + Qal *qatal* 1 c pl √קָבַע with 2 m s pronominal suf. On
וַאֲמַרְתֶּם, see note in 1:2. See note on בַּמֶּה in 2:17. The suffixing
qatal verb קְבַעֲנוּךָ is a recent perfective, translated in simple past
tense (WO 30.5.1b).

הַמַּעֲשֵׂר וְהַתְּרוּמָה: Def art with noun m s + *waw* cop with def
art and noun f s. This verbless clause is elliptical (implied meaning)
and emphatic, taking the force of a command (Hill, 306–7). For a
discussion on the meaning and significance of these two words, see
Glazier-McDonald, 189–91. *BHS* suggests two emendations. First, it
suggests adding the בְּ preposition to both nouns, following the Syriac,
Targums, and Vulgate texts (*BHS* note 8[d–d]). Second, *BHS* gives the
LXX addition of μεθ' ὑμῶν εἰσι meaning "are still with you" (*BHS*,
note 9[e]), which would make הַמַּעֲשֵׂר וְהַתְּרוּמָה the subject of the
clause. Both emendations are unnecessary for understanding the text
and the elliptical version with its emphatic nature makes better sense.
מַעֲשֵׂר is not an offering but an annual obligation paid to the temple
for support of sanctuary and its personnel (*NIDOT*, 2:1041). תְּרוּמָה
sometimes refers to Levitical offerings of which the priest could eat
a portion; however, the term can refer to any contribution or gift
given to the priests (*NIDOT*, 4:335–36). מַעֲשֵׂר and תְּרוּמָה are used
together only here and in Num 18:24.

בַּמְּאֵרָה֙ אַתֶּ֣ם נֵֽאָרִ֔ים וְאֹתִ֥י אַתֶּ֛ם קֹבְעִ֖ים הַגּ֥וֹי כֻּלּֽוֹ: 3:9

בַּמְּאֵרָה֙ אַתֶּ֣ם נֵֽאָרִ֔ים. ב prep with def art and noun f s + indep pers pron 2 m pl + Niph ptc m pl abs √אָרַר. This clause is a curse formula, using the strongest word for "curse" in the Hebrew Bible (see *TDOT*, 1:408–12). אָרַר is the antithesis of בָּרַךְ. See note on אָרַר in 2:2. The object/pronoun subject/verbal participle word order emphasizes both the object and the subject. The ב preposition indicates an internal accusative, translated "with" (WO §11.2.1g). The double use of the root אָרַר in its noun and verb form is also emphatic. Waltke and O'Connor call this construction an "internal cognate accusative" (WO §10.2.1g). אָרַר also occurs in 1:14 and 2:2. The use of the Niphal form occurs only here in the Hebrew Bible. Given the context of continuous wrongdoing by the priest and Israel, the Niphal should be translated as completed action with ongoing consequences "you are being cursed."

וְאֹתִ֥י אַתֶּ֛ם קֹבְעִ֖ים. *Waw* rel with the sign of dir obj and 1 c s pronominal suf + indep pers pron 2 m pl + Qal ptc m pl abs √קָבַע. This phrase is a repeat of the phrase in verse 8. The *waw* is epexegetical, indicating this clause clarifies the previous one (WO §39.2.4a, 4b). The *waw* epexegetical can be an emphatic *waw* (WO §39.2.4b), which may be translated "indeed" or left untranslated. The sign of the direct object is in the emphatic position, emphasizing that Yahweh (the speaker) is the one being robbed. אַתֶּם serves as the subject of the sentence. The Qal participle expresses continuous action, originating in the past and continuing into the future (see Stuart, 1368). See note in verse 8 on קָבַע.

הַגּ֥וֹי כֻּלּֽוֹ:. Def art with noun m s + noun m s constr with 3 m s pronominal suf. The phrase is an emphatic, verbless clause having the force of a command, paralleling the construction at the end of verse 8. I translated the clause as a singular emphatic clause with כֻּלּוֹ functioning as an adjective with the phrase meaning "the entire nation." However, this clause can be translated as a double emphatic, "the nation, all of it." The third singular suffix refers to הַגּוֹי. The use of הַגּוֹי for Israel instead of the more common עַם is probably intentional. הַגּוֹי is normally used of foreign nations and not Israel. Malachi's choice of words is perhaps sarcastic and definitely derogatory, indicating Israel has become like the other nations taking on their characteristics (*TDOT*, 2:429–33). Compare the usage of גּוֹי here and with its usage in 3:12, where גּוֹי refers to other nations and where the word order is reversed. *BHS* note 9[b–b] suggests this phrase is an addition, but Hill argues convincingly that reversal of the phrase in 3:12 is intentional and therefore requires הַגּוֹי כֻּלּוֹ to be a part of the original text (see Hill, 319).

3:10 הָבִ֣יאוּ אֶת־כָּל־הַֽמַּעֲשֵׂר֮ אֶל־בֵּ֣ית הָאוֹצָר֒ וִיהִ֤י טֶ֙רֶף֙ בְּבֵיתִ֔י וּבְחָנ֤וּנִי נָא֙ בָּזֹ֔את אָמַ֖ר יְהוָ֣ה צְבָא֑וֹת אִם־לֹ֧א אֶפְתַּ֣ח לָכֶ֗ם אֵ֚ת אֲרֻבּ֣וֹת הַשָּׁמַ֔יִם וַהֲרִיקֹתִ֥י לָכֶ֛ם בְּרָכָ֖ה עַד־בְּלִי־דָֽי׃

הָבִ֣יאוּ אֶת־כָּל־הַֽמַּעֲשֵׂר֮ אֶל־בֵּ֣ית הָאוֹצָר֒ וִיהִ֤י טֶ֙רֶף֙ בְּבֵיתִ֔י. Independent, imperative clause joined to a consequence or sequential clause.

הָבִ֣יאוּ. Hiph impv 2 m pl √בּוֹא. The Hiphil imperative is translated in the causative sense of "bring." This word occurs several times in chapter 3 in Qal form (vss 1, 2, 19, 23, 24) but only here in Hiphil.

אֶת־כָּל־הַֽמַּעֲשֵׂר. Sign of dir obj – noun m s constr – def art with noun m s. This construct genitive phrase is the object of הָבִ֣יאוּ.

אֶל־בֵּ֣ית הָאוֹצָר. Prep – noun m s constr + def art with noun m s. Construct genitive phrase functioning as the indirect object of the clause. The preposition אֶל has the sense of a goal or termination and is translated "into" (WO §11.2.2a).

וִיהִ֤י טֶ֙רֶף֙ בְּבֵיתִ֔י. *Waw* rel with Qal *yiqtol* 3 m s √הָיָה + noun m s + בְּ prep with noun m s constr and 1 c s pronominal suf. The Qal verb is a jussive form. The combination of the *waw* relative +

nonperfective verb following an imperative has a consequential force expressing result, translated "so that" (WO §34.4b). The meaning of טֶרֶף is debated. The word technically means "prey"; or that which is torn or plucked. On this basis, Glazier-McDonald cites Brichto who argues that the word indicates the priest are receiving inferior "food" from the people who are keeping the best for themselves (see GM, 193). However, given that the word can simply mean "food" and is used as such in Ps 111:5 and Prov 31:15. Given that this is a part of a command from Yahweh to bring that which has been held to Yahweh's house, then "food" is the appropriate meaning here (GM, 193–95; Stuart, 1370; Hill, 310; see *NIDOT*, 2:386). The בְּ preposition has a spatial sense of location (WO §11.2.5b). The writer uses בְּבֵיתִי as a synonymous term for הֵיכָל, perhaps emphasizing the intimate relationship between Yahweh and the Temple. However, בֵּית is a commonly used term for "temple" in post-exilic literature (GM, 195).

וּבְחָנוּנִי נָא בָּזֹאת אָמַר יְהוָה צְבָאוֹת. Imperative clause connected logically to the previous clause.

וּבְחָנוּנִי נָא בָּזֹאת. *Waw* conj with Qal impv 2 m pl √בָּחַן and 1 c s pronominal suf + part of entreaty + בְּ prep with demons adj. The conjunctive *waw* joins two independent, imperative clauses. The imperative, both here and in the previous clause, indicates urgency. בָּחַן occurs here and in 3:15 in Malachi. It is a nonspecific word for "testing" but has strong theological overtones. The word occurs mostly in poetic literature and in latter prophetic writings with Yahweh as the one doing the "testing." Testing Yahweh is usually condemned (as in Mal 3:15), but here Yahweh invites it as a demonstration of his faithfulness (*NIDOT*, 1:636–37). Stuart points out that the particle of entreaty does not have a softening effect on the imperative (Stuart, 1370–71) whereas Verhoef argues that it softens the command (Verhoef, 307). The particle of entreaty emphasizes the urgency of the command (Hill, 311). The demonstrative adjective is indefinite, referring to the manner of testing and is a nominal equivalent (WO §17.7.1a). The בְּ preposition has a circumstantial sense, meaning "in regards to" (WO §11.2.5e).

אָמַר יְהוָה צְבָאוֹת. Prophetic messenger formula placed in the middle of the verse perhaps to emphasize the authority giving the command.

אִם־לֹא אֶפְתַּח לָכֶם אֵת אֲרֻבּוֹת הַשָּׁמַיִם. This is a conditional dependent clause expressing consequential action.

אִם־לֹא אֶפְתַּח לָכֶם. Hypoth part – neg + Qal *yiqtol* 1 c s √פָּתַח + לְ prep with 2 m pl pronominal suf. אִם־לֹא can indicate the certainty of an oath or promise (GKC §149*a*), as is the case here. To the contrary, Keil and Delitzsch say this is an indirect question (KD, 659). The *yiqtol* verb indicates future action. לָכֶם is the indirect object of אֶפְתַּח. The לְ preposition has a sense of interest or advantage, indicating the recipients of the action (WO §11.2.10d).

אֵת אֲרֻבּוֹת הַשָּׁמַיִם. Sign of dir obj + noun f pl constr + def art with noun m pl. This genitival phrase is the direct object of אֶפְתַּח. Hill points out that "the phrase 'windows of heaven' is a poetic expression for drenching rainfall" (Hill, 314); therefore, it is an idiom.

וַהֲרִיקֹתִי לָכֶם בְּרָכָה עַד־בְּלִי־דָי׃. Consequential independent clause.

וַהֲרִיקֹתִי לָכֶם. Hiph *weqatal* 1 c s √ריק + לְ prep with 2 m pl pronominal suf. Waltke and O'Connor call the *waw* relative an apodosis *waw*, introducing an independent clause of consequence following a conditional dependent clause (WO §38.2b). The verb ריק only occurs in the Hiphil and Hophal, thus it is not causative here. לָכֶם is the indirect object and functions the same way it does earlier in this verse (see note above). The לְ preposition has a sense of interest or advantage, indicating the recipients of the action (WO §11.2.10d).

בְּרָכָה עַד־בְּלִי־דָי׃. Noun f s + prep – neg – subst. Direct object of וַהֲרִיקֹתִי. For information on בְּרָכָה, see note on בִּרְכוֹתֵיכֶם in 2:2. The phrase עַד־בְּלִי־דָי is unique to Malachi in the Masoretic Text and literally means, "until *there is* not sufficiency" (BDB, 191). The phrase is perhaps an idiom meaning "in abundance." Glazier-McDonald makes the argument that the word דָי meaning "sufficiency" equals "need"; therefore, the literal reading makes sense in that Yahweh will send rain until there is no more need for it (GM, 198).

3:11 וְגָעַרְתִּי לָכֶם בָּאֹכֵל וְלֹא־יַשְׁחִת לָכֶם אֶת־פְּרִי
הָאֲדָמָה וְלֹא־תְשַׁכֵּל לָכֶם הַגֶּפֶן בַּשָּׂדֶה אָמַר יְהוָה
צְבָאוֹת׃

Glazier-McDonald notes the syntactic parallel construction of verb + לָכֶם + noun (as direct object) at the end of 3:10 and three times in 3:11. She says this construction emphasizes the message as well as the continuity of the message (GM, 201).

וְגָעַרְתִּי לָכֶם בָּאֹכֵל. Qal *wᵉqatal* 1 c s √גָּעַר + לְ prep with 2 m pl pronominal suf + בְּ prep with def art and Qal act ptc m s abs √אָכַל. The *waw* relative continues the action of verse 10 in the future tense. The verb גָּעַר is used in 2:3 against the priests, but here demonstrates divine activity on behalf of the people.

לָכֶם. לְ preposition with the second masculine plural suffix occurs three times in this verse, all of which are the indirect objects of verbs. לָכֶם begins with a לְ preposition of interest or advantage, focusing attention on the indirect object of the verb (WO §11.2.10d), and being placed before the object.

בָּאֹכֵל. The preposition and Qal active participle is a substantive and functions as the direct object of וְגָעַרְתִּי. The verb גָּעַר with the בְּ preposition occurs ten of the fourteen times this word occurs in the Masoretic Text, where the בְּ preposition identifies the recipient of the "rebuke" (*TDOT*, 3:49). The preposition has an adversative sense, meaning "against," but can be left untranslated (WO §11.2.5d). The definite article with the preposition indicates a specific "devourer," perhaps locusts (GM, 199–200; KD, 660; Verhoef, 308), but one that is not identified in Malachi.

וְלֹא־יַשְׁחִת לָכֶם אֶת־פְּרִי הָאֲדָמָה. This is a clause of conse-quence or the result of divine action of the previous clause. The *waw* can be translated "so that" (see Stuart, 1365 and Hill, 291.)

וְלֹא־יַשְׁחִת לָכֶם. *Waw* conj with neg – Hiph *yiqtol* 3 m s √שָׁחַת + לְ prep with 2 m pl pronominal suf. The *waw* relative functions as a connector to the previous clause showing consequence. The nonper-fective verb indicates the action is continued from the previous clause and in future time. The לְ preposition of interest marks the indirect object (WO §11.2.10d).

אֶת־פְּרִי הָאֲדָמָה. Sign of dir obj – noun m s constr + def art with noun f s. The two nouns form a construct phrase. This is a com-mon phrase in the Hebrew Bible referring to crops, occurring fre-quently in Deuteronomy (7:13; 26:2, 10; 28:4, 11; etc.).

וְלֹא־תְשַׁכֵּל לָכֶם הַגֶּפֶן בַּשָּׂדֶה אָמַר יְהוָה צְבָאוֹת׃. This clause is parallel in syntax and thought to the previous clause.

וְלֹא־תְשַׁכֵּל לָכֶם. *Waw* conj with neg – Pi *yiqtol* 3 f s √שָׁכַל + לְ prep with 2 m pl pronominal suf. The *waw* conjunction and the negative particle here introduce a second clause of negative result. The Piel form of the verb שָׁכַל intensifies the meaning to "make childless" or "cause barrenness," thereby strengthening the curse (BDB, 1013). The idea here is that the "fruit of the ground" will not be barren but be able to ripen (GM, 201). The לְ preposition has a sense of interest or advantage, indicating the recipients of the action (WO §11.2.10d).

הַגֶּפֶן בַּשָּׂדֶה. Def art with noun f s + בְּ prep with noun m s. The noun הַגֶּפֶן acts as a collective singular representing all fruit bear-ing plants. The prepositional phrase בַּשָּׂדֶה, also a collective singular, modifies הַגֶּפֶן.

אָמַר יְהוָה צְבָאוֹת׃. Prophetic messenger formula.

3:12 וְאִשְּׁרוּ אֶתְכֶם כָּל־הַגּוֹיִם כִּי־תִהְיוּ אַתֶּם אֶרֶץ חֵפֶץ אָמַר יְהוָה צְבָאוֹת׃

וְאִשְּׁרוּ אֶתְכֶם כָּל־הַגּוֹיִם. Pi *wᵉqatal* 3 c pl √אָשַׁר + sign of dir obj with 2 m pl pronominal suf + noun m s constr – def art with noun m pl abs. The *waw* conjunction and the *qatal* verb indicate a clause of consequent situation in future time (WO §32.2.3a), translated "then."

אֶתְכֶם. Dir obj of וְאִשְּׁרוּ.

כָּל־הַגּוֹיִם. Subj of וְאִשְּׁרוּ. The Hebrew words here are reversed from their occurrence in 3:9, perhaps a syntactical indication of the reversal of fortune for the people of Israel (Hill, 319).

כִּי־תִהְיוּ אַתֶּם אֶרֶץ חֵפֶץ אָמַר יְהוָה צְבָאוֹת: Subordinate clause of logical sequence.

כִּי־תִהְיוּ אַתֶּם אֶרֶץ חֵפֶץ. Conj – Qal *yiqtol* 2 m pl √הָיָה + per pron 2 m pl + noun f s constr + noun m s. The *yiqtol* verb continues the action in future time. The personal pronoun אַתֶּם functions as the subject and has been added for emphasis. אֶרֶץ חֵפֶץ is either an attributive noun + adjective in an accusative phrase meaning "delight-ful land" or it can be a genitival phrase with a construct noun preceding an absolute noun, meaning "land of delight." I have translated it as a construct noun phrase, as the vowel pointing for חֵפֶץ is for a noun rather than an adjective. See notes on חֵפֶץ in 1:10; 2:17; and 3:1.

אָמַר יְהוָה צְבָאוֹת: Prophetic messenger formula, effectively ending the fifth oracle.

Sixth Oracle: Hope for the Community (3:13-21)

Malachi 3:13-21

13 "Your words have been strong against me," says Yahweh, "but you say, 'What have we spoken against you?' 14 You have said, '[It is] vanity to serve God and for what profit? For we keep his charge but we walk mournfully in the presence of Yahweh of hosts. 15 And now we call arrogant ones blessed. Indeed, evildoers have been built up. They even tested God and they escaped!'"

16 Then the fearers of Yahweh spoke, each one with his friend, and Yahweh paid attention and he listened. Then, a book of remembrance was written in his presence for the fearers of Yahweh and for the ones who highly regard his name.

17 "And they will be mine," says Yahweh of hosts, "a possession on the day when I act and I will show compassion upon them just as a parent shows compassion upon his child, the one who serves him. 18 And again, you will discern between a righteous one and a wicked one, between one who serves God and one not serving him. 19 For behold, the day is coming, burning as the oven, and all the insolent ones and the evildoers will be stubble. And the coming day will set them ablaze," says Yahweh of hosts, "so that it will leave for them neither a root nor a branch. 20 But a sun of righteousness will rise for you, fearers of my name, and healing [will be] in its wings. And you will go out and you will jump around like calves of a stall. 21 Then you will tread down evildoers for they will be ashes under the soles of your feet on that day when I act," says Yahweh of hosts.

The final oracle continues the prophetic disputation in the pseudo-dialogue, question and answer format. Yahweh speaks in first person, as in most of the oracles. However, verse 16 interrupts the first person speech with a narrative discourse written from the perspective of a narrator, not Yahweh. The writer employs opposites (such as צַדִּיק and רָשָׁע) and uses metaphors and similes more in this oracle than in previous ones.

Key Words					
הַיּוֹם	חָזַק	צַדִּיק	רָשָׁע	שׁוּב	שָׁמַר

3:13 חֲזְקוּ עָלַי דִּבְרֵיכֶם אָמַר יְהוָה וַאֲמַרְתֶּם מַה־נִּדְבַּרְנוּ
עָלֶיךָ:

חֲזְקוּ עָלַי דִּבְרֵיכֶם. Qal *qatal* 3 m pl √חָזַק + prep with 1 c s pronominal suf + noun m pl constr with 2 m pl pronominal suf. Stuart points out that the combination עַל + דָּבָר + חָזַק is found in 2 Sam 24:4 and 1 Chron 21:4 where חָזַק means "overpower" or "overrule" (Stuart, 1374). The preposition עַל is in opposition to the subject and should be translated "against" (see WO §11.2.13f).

אָמַר יְהוָה. Abbreviated messenger formula separating two clauses and placed here to emphasize the authority behind the message. *BHS* note 13ª suggests inserting צְבָאוֹת to complete the messenger formula as it regularly occurs in Malachi. However, Hill points out that the shorter version used here and in 1:2 "marks a type of envelope construction framing the six disputations" (Hill, 330), thus the emendation is unnecessary.

וַאֲמַרְתֶּם מַה־נִּדְבַּרְנוּ עָלֶיךָ:. Discourse with an emphatic interrogative clause giving the people's response to the accusation of the previous clause.

וַאֲמַרְתֶּם. Qal *weqatal* 2 m pl √אָמַר. Same construction as in 1:2, 6; 2:14, 17; 3:7, 8. See note in 1:2.

מַה־נִּדְבַּרְנוּ עָלֶיךָ:. Interrog – Niph *qatal* 1 c pl √דָּבַר + prep with 2 m s pronominal suf. Hill, citing WO §18.3f, translates the interrogative "how" as one of exclamatory force (Hill, 330), however,

I have kept the more common translation of "what" which seems to fit the statement better (as with Stuart, 1373; Verhoef, 312; GM, 209; and KD, 660). The verb form has the same root as the noun of the previous clause (also with the preposition that follows), emphasizing the close parallel of the people's response to the accusation. The second masculine singular pronoun is the indirect object of the verb.

3:14 אֲמַרְתֶּ֗ם שָׁ֚וְא עֲבֹ֣ד אֱלֹהִ֔ים וּמַה־בֶּ֗צַע כִּ֤י שָׁמַ֨רְנוּ֙
מִשְׁמַרְתּ֔וֹ וְכִ֤י הָלַ֨כְנוּ֙ קְדֹ֣רַנִּ֔ית מִפְּנֵ֖י יְהוָ֥ה צְבָאֽוֹת׃

אֲמַרְתֶּ֗ם שָׁ֚וְא עֲבֹ֣ד אֱלֹהִ֔ים וּמַה־בֶּ֗צַע. The clause is a reply to the people's question in the previous verse.

אֲמַרְתֶּ֗ם. Qal *qatal* 2 m pl √אָמַר. The perfective verb continues the past tense of the Niphal verb in the previous question. The prophet has left off a coordinating conjunction, as one expects to find on this clause to mark the change in speakers.

שָׁ֚וְא עֲבֹ֣ד אֱלֹהִ֔ים. Noun m s + Qal inf constr √עָבַד + noun m pl. The translation of the phrase is straightforward; however, this use of the infinitive is not common in Malachi. Hill notes that the verb עָבַד functions as the predicate of the clause and has the sense of a participle (Hill, 332). Stuart suggests that this phrase may have been a common saying, a proverb, in postexilic Israel (Stuart, 1378).

וּמַה־בֶּ֗צַע. *Waw* conj with interrog – noun m s. The *waw* is conjunctive, joining the two related clauses (see WO §39.25a). The interrogative is followed by a dagesh forte conjunctive (see GKC §37b). The verbal from of the noun בֶּצַע was a technical term meaning "to cut off" as one cuts cloth from a loom. However, the term evolved to mean "to profit," and usually is used in a pejorative sense of illegal profit or unjust gain (*TDOT*, 2:206–7). Here the term is neutral in meaning.

כִּ֤י שָׁמַ֨רְנוּ֙ מִשְׁמַרְתּ֔וֹ. Conj + Qal *qatal* 1 c pl √שָׁמַר + noun f s constr with 3 m s pronominal suf. The coordinating conjunction

כִּי joins this clause with the previous one and has a logical sense. כִּי is translated "for" (WO §39.3.4e). The clause uses the verb/noun combination of the same root, שמר, which is often referred to as an internal adjunct. This pairing of שמר is common in the Pentateuch as an idiom of obedience to Yahweh's law (e.g., Gen 26:5; Lev 8:35; Num 8:26; and Deut 11:1). שָׁמַר has the notion of diligent respect for religious responsibilities (*NIDOT* 4:183).

מִשְׁמַרְתּוֹ. Dir obj of שָׁמַרְנוּ.

וְכִי הָלַכְנוּ קְדֹרַנִּית מִפְּנֵי יְהוָה צְבָאוֹת: Relative clause with a logical sense and continues the thought of the previous clause.

וְכִי הָלַכְנוּ קְדֹרַנִּית. *Waw* conj with conjunctive adv + Qal *qatal* 1 c pl √הָלַךְ + adv. The *waw* functions as a coordinating conjunction with an alternative force and is translated "but." The word order here is the same as the previous clause and should be translated in the same manner. קְדֹרַנִּית only occurs here in the Hebrew Bible and is often translated "as mourners" based upon the root קָדַר which means "to be dark" (BDB, 871). However, with the lack of the preposition כְּ, the word should be translated as an adverb "mournfully."

מִפְּנֵי יְהוָה צְבָאוֹת:. Prep with noun m pl constr + divine title. The combination of the preposition מִן and the noun פָּנֶה is a "frozen union," according to Waltke and O'Connor, with a locative sense and has the meaning of "in the presence of" (BDB, 818; WO §11.3.1a). This phrase is a near parallel to the prophetic messenger formula commonly found in Malachi.

3:15 וְעַתָּה אֲנַחְנוּ מְאַשְּׁרִים זֵדִים גַּם־נִבְנוּ עֹשֵׂי רִשְׁעָה
גַּם בָּחֲנוּ אֱלֹהִים וַיִּמָּלֵטוּ:

וְעַתָּה אֲנַחְנוּ מְאַשְּׁרִים זֵדִים. Temporal transitioning, verbless clause bringing the action from the past to the present.

וְעַתָּה. *Waw* conj with temporal adv. The *waw* conjunction is a sequential *waw* and coordinates this clause with the previous one. The *waw* + עַתָּה has a logical force and creates a juxtaposition between then and now (WO §39.3.1h).

אֲנַ֫חְנוּ. Indep pers pron 1 c pl. אֲנַ֫חְנוּ functions as the subject of the clause.

מְאַשְּׁרִים זֵדִים. Pi ptc m pl abs √אָשַׁר + adj m pl. The participle is the predicate of the clause and has the sense of continuous action in present time. זֵדִים is the direct object of the clause. It functions as a substantive and is an accusative of specification (Hill, 335). The word also occurs in 3:19.

גַּם־נִבְנוּ֙ עֹשֵׂי רִשְׁעָ֔ה. The coordinating adverb גַּם begins this and the next clause, indicating a close connection with the previous clause (see WO §39.3.4d), perhaps having an emphatic sense. Glazier-McDonald points out that when גַּם introduces intensive clauses, it often makes the clause emphatic (GM, 214). Alternately, Hill suggests גם beginning these two clauses is disjunctive and should be translated "not only . . . but also" (Hill, 336; Niccacci, 98).

נִבְנוּ. Niph *qatal* 3 c pl √בָּנָה. בָּנָה literally means "to be built up" but has a figurative sense here meaning "prosper."

עֹשֵׂי רִשְׁעָה. Noun m pl constr + noun f s. Construct genitive phrase that is the subject of נִבְנוּ. רִשְׁעָה contains a variety of meanings including "wickedness," "evil intent," and "injustice." Various forms of this word are common in wisdom literature (*NIDOT*, 3:1201). The broader context of Malachi suggests רִשְׁעָה here refers to those who do not keep the covenant. The word רִשְׁעָה also occurs in 1:4 and 3:19.

גַּם בָּחֲנוּ אֱלֹהִים וַיִּמָּלֵטוּ׃. Adverbial clause expanding the thought of the previous clause. Waltke and O'Connor note that גַּם can mark the climax of an exposition (WO §39.3.4d), as it perhaps does here.

בָּחֲנוּ. Qal *qatal* 3 c pl √בָּחַן. The implied subject of the verb is עֹשֵׂי רִשְׁעָה.

אֱלֹהִים. Obj of בָּחֲנוּ.

וַיִּמָּלֵֽטוּ׃. Niph *wayyiqtol* 3 m pl מָלַט√. The *waw* consecutive coordinates the action with the previous clause. In this case, the action of the verb is the result of the action of the previous clause. The *wayyiqtol* form following a *qatal* form can have the temporal sense of the *qatal*, in this case past tense and meaning "escaped" (WO §33.3.1c).

3:16 אָז נִדְבְּרוּ יִרְאֵי יְהוָה אִישׁ אֶת־רֵעֵהוּ וַיַּקְשֵׁב יְהוָה
וַיִּשְׁמָע וַיִּכָּתֵב סֵפֶר זִכָּרוֹן לְפָנָיו לְיִרְאֵי יְהוָה
וּלְחֹשְׁבֵי שְׁמֽוֹ׃

The prophetic disputation changes to narrative in verse 16 and then changes back to prophetic disputation in verse 17. Hill points out that this narrative interruption is unique here in Malachi (Hill, 337). A few scholars view this interruption as evidence that the verse is a later addition (see Merrill, 381). While this may possible, there is no textual witness suggesting verse 16 is a later addition.

אָז נִדְבְּרוּ יִרְאֵי יְהוָה אִישׁ אֶת־רֵעֵהוּ. Temporal clause of sequence, connected in thought to the previous verse.

אָז נִדְבְּרוּ. Adv + Niph *qatal* 3 c pl דָּבַר√. The temporal adverb אָז has a logical force continuing a sequence of events (WO §39.3.4f). *BHS* suggests emending the text to read with the LXX, which translates אָז with ταῦτα "this" (see *BHS* note 16ᵃ). However, the Masoretic Text makes sense and does not require emendation. The Niphal verb is reflexive in nature, as indicated by the phrase יִרְאֵי יְהוָה (see Smith, 336, note 16.a).

יִרְאֵי יְהוָה. Noun m pl constr + pr noun. The genitival phrase is the subject of נִדְבְּרוּ. Many scholars translate יִרְאֵי as a participle but it probably should be read as a noun.

אִישׁ אֶת־רֵעֵהוּ. Noun m s + prep – noun m s constr with 3 m s pronominal suf. The phrase is an idiom of reciprocity, common in the Hebrew Bible (e.g., Exod 21:18; 1 Sam 20:41 [2x]; and 2 Kgs 3:23). The singular nouns are used in a collective sense.

וַיַּקְשֵׁב יְהוָה וַיִּשְׁמָע. Qal *wayyiqtol* 3 m s √קָשַׁע + pr noun + Qal *wayyiqtol* 3 m s √שָׁמַע. יְהוָה serves as the subject of both verbs. The *waw* relative (*waw* consecutive) on וַיַּקְשֵׁב connects the action from the previous clause to this clause. The *waw* relative on וַיִּשְׁמָע is conjunctive and continues the mood of the sequence.

וַיִּכָּתֵב סֵפֶר זִכָּרוֹן לְפָנָיו לְיִרְאֵי יְהוָה וּלְחֹשְׁבֵי שְׁמוֹ: Relative clause continuing the action of the previous clause.

וַיִּכָּתֵב. Niph *wayyiqtol* 3 m s √כָּתַב. The *waw* relative with the nonperfective verb indicates a continuation of action from the previous clause. It is translated "then."

סֵפֶר זִכָּרוֹן. Noun m s constr + noun m s. This construct genitival phrase is the subject of וַיִּכָּתֵב. This phrase only occurs here in the Hebrew Bible. A similar phrase is in Esther 6:1.

לְפָנָיו. לְ prep with noun m pl constr and 3 m s pronominal suf. The preposition and noun combination are "a frozen union" (WO §11.3.1a) forming an independent word that has a spatial sense, meaning "before."

לְיִרְאֵי יְהוָה וּלְחֹשְׁבֵי שְׁמוֹ: לְ prep with noun m pl constr + pr noun + conj with לְ prep and Qal act ptc m pl const √חָשַׁב + noun m s constr with 3 m s pronominal suf. These parallel genitival phrases are parallel in thought (referring to the same persons and stated twice for emphasis). Both phrases function as the indirect objects of וַיִּכָּתֵב. Both לְ prepositions are a *lameds* of interest (WO §11.2.10d). The construct participle in the second phase functions as a noun, the same as the construct noun of the first phrase. *BHS* note 16[b–b] suggests emending the last phrase to וּלְחֹסֵי בִשְׁמוֹ, which means "and the ones who seeks refuge in his name." This emendation is not necessary. The word חָשַׁב is usually translated "think" but can mean "esteem" or "regard" (BDB, 363; *HALOT*, 360). This latter definition makes sense in this context and therefore חָשַׁב should be retained.

3:17 וְהָיוּ לִי אָמַר יְהוָה צְבָאוֹת לַיּוֹם אֲשֶׁר אֲנִי עֹשֶׂה
סְגֻלָּה וְחָמַלְתִּי עֲלֵיהֶם כַּאֲשֶׁר יַחְמֹל אִישׁ עַל־בְּנוֹ
הָעֹבֵד אֹתוֹ:

The text changes from narrative discourse back to prophetic disputation in verse 17 with Yahweh's speech.

וְהָיוּ לִי אָמַר יְהוָה צְבָאוֹת לַיּוֹם אֲשֶׁר אֲנִי עֹשֶׂה סְגֻלָּה.
Independent, declarative clause.

וְהָיוּ לִי. Qal *we qatal* 3 c pl √הָיָה + לְ prep with 1 c s pronominal
suf. This is an independent clause showing possession. The *waw* relative with the perfective form of הָיָה usually has a deictic temporal
function and should be translated in future time (WO §32.2.6c).
Similarly, Merwe notes that the *we qatal* form, *waw* consecutive + perfect, "indicates the backbone of predictive discourse" (MNK, 169),
hence a translation in future time. The series of *we qatal* forms in 3:17
and 18 are of this nature. לְ + הָיָה preposition is a periphrastic idiom
showing possession (*TDOT*, 3:372).

אָמַר יְהוָה צְבָאוֹת. Prophetic messenger formula.

לְ. לַיּוֹם אֲשֶׁר אֲנִי עֹשֶׂה סְגֻלָּה prep with noun m s + rel pron
+ indep pers pron 1 c s + Qal act ptc m s abs √עָשָׂה + noun f s. This
is a subordinate clause describing וְהָיוּ לִי. The לְ preposition has a
temporal sense (WO §11.2.10c). לַיּוֹם has the preposition added to
הַיּוֹם. הַיּוֹם has significant theological meaning and emphasizes the
importance of the coming event. It indicates a decisive point in time
where Yahweh's actions will permanently change the course of events
(*NIDOT*, 2:423). Hill connects הַיּוֹם with the "day of the Lord." He
says the prophet borrows לַיּוֹם from Ezekiel (30:2) and Joel (1:15)
where both texts tell of a coming day of Yahweh's judgment (Hill,
341). This is a common theme in the fourth and sixth oracles and
in the appendix (in 3:23). The relative pronoun אֲשֶׁר has a temporal
function meaning "when" and introduces a relative clause describing לַיּוֹם. אֲנִי is the subject of עֹשֶׂה. The participle עֹשֶׂה describes a

present, pending action. עָשָׂה has the same meaning of "act" here, as it does in 3:21 (see *CHAL*, 285; also for verse 21). Stuart says עָשָׂה is used here as an intransitive verb (not taking an object), therefore the word following cannot be an object but rather the subject of the clause (Stuart, 1383–84). However, the preferred reading makes סְגֻלָּה the predicate of וְהָיוּ, which is interrupted here by the messenger formula. Hill points out that many English translations assume a gapping of לִי from the preceding independent clause and translate the pronoun as possessive "my possession" (Hill, 324). סְגֻלָּה is a word found in the Pentateuch (Exod 19:5; Deut 7:6; 14:2; and 26:18) but absent from prophetic literature except here. It is covenantal terminology used in the Pentateuch solely of Yahweh's possession. The word is used once in 1 Chron 29:3 of one's personal property.

וְחָמַלְתִּי עֲלֵיהֶם כַּאֲשֶׁר יַחְמֹל אִישׁ עַל־בְּנוֹ הָעֹבֵד אֹתוֹ. Epexegetical clause, giving additional information about the previous clause.

וְחָמַלְתִּי עֲלֵיהֶם. Qal *wᵉqatal* 1 c s √חָמַל + prep with 3 m pl pronominal suf. The *wᵉqatal* continues the action in future time. The verb חָמַל frequently is paired with עַל (Hill, 343), meaning "have compassion upon." This clause has an epexegetical function, describing the action of Yahweh introduced with וְהָיוּ in the clause above. The עַל preposition governs the object of interest, translated "on" or "upon" (WO §11.2.13c).

כַּאֲשֶׁר יַחְמֹל אִישׁ עַל־בְּנוֹ הָעֹבֵד אֹתוֹ. Rel pron + Qal *yiqtol* 3 m s √חָמַל + noun m s + prep – noun m s constr with 3 m s pronominal suf + def art with Qal act ptc m s abs √עָבַד + sign of dir obj with 3 m s pronominal suf. The grammar of the comparative clause is straightforward with a verb/subject/object/modifier word order. The relative pronoun אֲשֶׁר with the כְּ preposition introduces a clause of comparison and is translated "as" (WO §38.5a). The prophet uses the same verb חָמַל as in the previous clause so that the reader clearly understands what is compared. אִישׁ is the subject of the clause. It is indefinite here and is a noun of class (WO §13.8b). The prophet echoes the wording in 1:6, creating a contrasting parallel between the two passages. The phrase אִישׁ עַל־בְּנוֹ uses masculine nouns but should be understood as gender nonspecific, i.e., "parent" and "child" (see WO §6.5.3). הָעֹבֵד אֹתוֹ is a dependent relative clause functioning as an attributive adjective and it modifies בְּנוֹ.

3:18 וְשַׁבְתֶּם וּרְאִיתֶם בֵּין צַדִּיק לְרָשָׁע בֵּין עֹבֵד אֱלֹהִים
לַאֲשֶׁר לֹא עֲבָדוֹ:

Verse 18 continues the sequential action of verse 17.

וְשַׁבְתֶּם וּרְאִיתֶם בֵּין צַדִּיק לְרָשָׁע. Clause of consequence connected in thought to the first clause of verse 17.

וְשַׁבְתֶּם. Qal wᵉqatal 2 m pl √שׁוּב. The qatal verb may be an auxiliary and function as an adverb, translated "and again" (WO §39.3.1b; so GM, 228; Hill, 326; and Verhoef, 312). See a similar construction with וְנָשׁוּב וְנִבְנֶה in 1:4 above and see note on שׁוּב in 3:10. However, the context allows the verb to be translated "and you will turn" having the sense of repenting.

וּרְאִיתֶם. Qal wᵉqatal 2 m pl √רָאָה. The waw is conjunctive, joining the two wᵉqatal verbs and continuing the sequence of future actions.

בֵּין צַדִּיק לְרָשָׁע. Prep + noun m s + לְ prep with noun m s. This phrase is the first of two parallel phrases expressing contrast. The preposition בֵּין + לְ preposition have an exclusive sense, expressing distinction (WO §11.2.6c). צַדִּיק לְרָשָׁע are collective singular nouns and are contrasted using the לְ preposition as polar opposites. צַדִּיק implies "behaving in a right order in the community and before God" and has the notion of how one should act for a secure and beneficent future (NIDOT, 3:766). For information on the meaning of רָשָׁע, see note on רְשָׁעָה in 3:15.

בֵּין עֹבֵד אֱלֹהִים לַאֲשֶׁר לֹא עֲבָדוֹ:. Prep + Qal act ptc m s abs √עָבַד + noun m pl + לְ prep with rel pron + neg + Qal qatal 3 m s √עָבַד with 3 m s pronominal suf. This phrase is parallel in thought and order with the previous phrase. The parallel construction is for emphasis.

עֲבָדֹו . . . עָבֵד. The participle has a relative use in present time. עֲבָדֹו can be a noun masculine singular with a third masculine singular pronominal suffix or Qal *qatal* third masculine singular with a third masculine singular pronominal suffix. The form probably is a verb with the suffix functioning as the object. The *qatal* form here is a persistent perfect, indicating an action that began in the past but continues into the present (WO §30.5.1c). Both uses of עָבַד here echo the usage of the same word in 1:6 and 3:17, placing emphasis upon "serving" as a criterion for righteousness.

אֱלֹהִים. Dir obj of עָבַד.

לַאֲשֶׁר. The לְ preposition with the relative pronoun אֲשֶׁר is infrequent in the Hebrew Bible, occurring 24 times. Hill points out, however, that the לְ preposition when combined with the preposition בֵּין functions like a *waw* copulative, translated "between . . . and one who . . ." (Hill, 345).

3:19   כִּי־הִנֵּה הַיֹּום בָּא בֹּעֵר כַּתַּנּוּר וְהָיֽוּ כָל־זֵדִים וְכָל־ עֹשֵׂה רִשְׁעָה קַשׁ וְלִהַט אֹתָם הַיֹּום הַבָּא אָמַר יְהוָה צְבָאֹות אֲשֶׁר לֹא־יַעֲזֹב לָהֶם שֹׁרֶשׁ וְעָנָֽף:

כִּי־הִנֵּה הַיֹּום בָּא בֹּעֵר כַּתַּנּוּר. Emphatic and temporal subordinate clause of pending action.

כִּי־הִנֵּה הַיֹּום בָּא. Conj – demons part + def art with noun m s + Qal act ptc m s abs √בֹוא. The conjunctive adverb כִּי has a logical force and is translated "for" (WO §39.3.4e). The particle הִנֵּה adds immediacy to and certainty of the coming event. Hill points out that the combination of the adverb כִּי + emphatic particle הִנֵּה + participle is a common announcement formula of something about to happen

(Hill, 345). However, Stuart argues that the particle does not indicate immediacy but rather definiteness that the event will occur (Stuart, 1386). The definite article with the noun יוֹם in reference to Yahweh's judgment is an allusion to the longer phrase יוֹם יְהוָה, a key phrase in prophetic literature (as used in 3:23 below). The participle functions as a predicate of immediate, impending action (see WO §37.6f). See note on לַיּוֹם in 3:17.

בֹּעֵר כַּתַּנּוּר. Qal act ptc m s abs √בָּעַר + כְּ prep with def art and noun m s. This phrase is a metaphor describing the coming day, perhaps echoing Ps 21:10 and Hosea 7:6. The participle functions as the predicate of the clause. The כְּ preposition is a comparative (WO §11.2.9b(3)). The LXX *Graecus originalis* adds φλέξει αὐτούς meaning "and it consumes them"; however, the addition is not necessary (see *BHS* note 19[a]).

וְהָיוּ כָל־זֵדִים וְכָל־עֹשֵׂה רִשְׁעָה קַשׁ. Relative clause continuing the action of the previous clause.

וְהָיוּ. Qal *weqatal* 3 m pl √הָיָה. The *waw* relative indicating sequence with the perfective form of הָיָה usually has a deictic temporal function and should be translated in future time (WO §32.2.6c). Merwe calls the *weqatal* form a predictive perfect (MNK, 169). See note on the same word in 3:17.

כָל־זֵדִים וְכָל־עֹשֵׂה רִשְׁעָה. Noun m s constr – adj m pl + conj with noun m s constr – Qal act ptc m s abs √עָשָׂה + noun f s. The noun כֹּל is a quantifier representing totality (WO §9.5.3f). The prophet uses זֵדִים and רִשְׁעָה purposefully here to draw a close connection with their usage in 3:15. *BHS* note 19[b] suggests emending the text to read עֹשֵׂי instead of עֹשֵׂה, making the participle construct. Given the same phrase occurs in 3:15 in construct form and that the absolute form makes little sense in its context, I agree with emending the text.

קַשׁ. Noun m s. Predicate nominative of וְהָיוּ. קַשׁ is a word commonly used in metaphors referring to Yahweh's judgment (e.g., Isa 5:24).

וְלִהַט אֹתָם הַיּוֹם הַבָּא אָמַר יְהוָה צְבָאוֹת אֲשֶׁר לֹא־
יַעֲזֹב לָהֶם שֹׁרֶשׁ וְעָנָף: Independent clause continuing the
sequence of events in future time.

וְלִהַט אֹתָם הַיּוֹם הַבָּא. Pi *we qatal* 3 m s √לָהַט + sign of dir
obj with 3 m pl pronominal suf + def art with noun m s + def art with
Qal act ptc m s abs √בּוֹא. The *we qatal* form continues the action in
future time. The Piel form intensifies the verb indicating complete
consumption of the blaze. The third person plural pronominal suffix
is the direct object of וְלִהַט and refers to "all the insolent ones and evil
doers" stated earlier in the verse. The phrase הַיּוֹם הַבָּא is the subject
of וְלִהַט. See note above on הַיּוֹם.

אָמַר יְהוָה צְבָאוֹת. Prophetic messenger formula.

אֲשֶׁר לֹא־יַעֲזֹב לָהֶם שֹׁרֶשׁ וְעָנָף: Rel pron + neg – Qal
yiqtol 3 m s √עָזַב + לְ + prep with 3 m pl pronominal suf + noun m s +
waw cop with noun m s. Dependent, consequential clause descriptive
of הַיּוֹם and translated "so that." The negative and the nonperfective
verb regulate two objects, שֹׁרֶשׁ and עָנָף. The לְ preposition is a *lamed*
of disadvantage and marks the indirect object (WO §11.2.10d).

3:20 וְזָרְחָה לָכֶם יִרְאֵי שְׁמִי שֶׁמֶשׁ צְדָקָה וּמַרְפֵּא בִּכְנָפֶיהָ
וִיצָאתֶם וּפִשְׁתֶּם כְּעֶגְלֵי מַרְבֵּק:

וְזָרְחָה לָכֶם יִרְאֵי שְׁמִי שֶׁמֶשׁ צְדָקָה וּמַרְפֵּא בִּכְנָפֶיהָ.
The *waw* relative joins this independent clause with the previous ones
and continues the action in the future tense.

וְזָרְחָה לָכֶם. Qal *we qatal* 3 f s √זָרַח + לְ + prep with 2 m pl pronominal suf. The *waw* conjunction continues the action from the previous verses but is often translated as an adversative "but" marking a
transition in the object of the action to the righteous ones. The verb
here is feminine because the subject שֶׁמֶשׁ צְדָקָה is feminine. The לְ
preposition is a *lamed* of interest, which Waltke and O'Connor call an
ethical dative (see WO §11.2.10d; GKC 119*s*). The second masculine
plural suffix is the indirect object of וְזָרְחָה.

יִרְאֵי שְׁמִי. Qal act ptc m pl constr √יָרֵא + noun m s constr with 1 c s pronominal suf. This phrase modifies the pronominal suffix לָכֶם. The wording here is closely connected with parallel words in 3:16. Also, those referenced here are opposite of those in 1:6, "despisers of my name." This reference, in conjunction with other similar wording in 1:6 and 3:19, has an enveloping effect for the entire book.

שֶׁמֶשׁ צְדָקָה. Noun m s constr + noun f s. The genitival phrase is the subject of וְזָרְחָה. This phrase is found only here in the Hebrew Bible. The translation above understands the phrase as indefinite, following the technical construction of the phrase (with Hill, 326; Petersen, 219; but contra Stuart, 1381; GM, 206; Verhoef, 312; Smith, 336; and KD, 662). See Verhoef 327–29 for a technical/theological discussion of this phrase. The phrase is perhaps an idiom of the ancient winged sun disk (see Hill, 350).

וּמַרְפֵּא בִּכְנָפֶיהָ. Waw conj with noun m s + בְּ prep with noun f dual constr and 3 f s pronominal suf. The waw is epexegetical, further clarifying שֶׁמֶשׁ צְדָקָה, and continuing the metaphor. The בְּ preposition has a spatial sense (WO §11.2.5b). Although the phrase offers no translation difficulties, it is unique to here in the Hebrew Bible, which makes its interpretation difficult.

וִיצָאתֶם וּפִשְׁתֶּם כְּעֶגְלֵי מַרְבֵּק׃. The waw relative joins this clause of consequence with the previous clause.

וִיצָאתֶם. Qal weqatal 2 m pl √יָצָא. The weqatal form continues the future tense of the previous clause (MNK, 169).

וּפִשְׁתֶּם. Qal weqatal 2 m pl √פּוּשׁ. The waw is a simple conjunction, joining the two verbs. The verb פּוּשׁ is rare in the Hebrew Bible and is found only in Jer 50:11; Hab 1:8; and Mal 3:20 (BDB, 807).

כְּעֶגְלֵי מַרְבֵּק׃. כְּ prep with noun m pl constr + noun m s. The genitival phrase is indefinite. The כְּ preposition has a comparative sense (WO §11.2.9b). The phrase is a metaphor, with the image of the fatted calf as symbolic of prosperity of divine blessing (Hill, 353).

3:21 וַעֲסוֹתֶם רְשָׁעִים כִּי־יִהְיוּ אֵפֶר תַּחַת כַּפּוֹת רַגְלֵיכֶם
בַּיּוֹם אֲשֶׁר אֲנִי עֹשֶׂה אָמַר יְהוָה צְבָאוֹת:

וַעֲסוֹתֶם רְשָׁעִים. Qal *we qatal* 2 m pl √עסס + adj m pl. *Waw* relative continues the action in future time. The verb is unique to here in the Hebrew Bible (BDB, 779; *HALOT*, 861) although the noun form, meaning "sweet wine," is found in Isa 49:26; Joel 1:5; and 4:18. רְשָׁעִים is the object of וַעֲסוֹתֶם.

כִּי־יִהְיוּ אֵפֶר תַּחַת כַּפּוֹת רַגְלֵיכֶם בַּיּוֹם אֲשֶׁר אֲנִי עֹשֶׂה. This dependent clause modifies רְשָׁעִים in the previous clause.

כִּי־יִהְיוּ אֵפֶר. Conj – Qal *yiqtol* 3 m pl √הָיָה + noun m s. The nonperfective verb continues the future tense of the discourse. The כִּי conjunction introduces the subordinate clause and is translated "for." However, Hill opts for interpreting כִּי as an emphatic clausal adverb, translated "indeed" (Hill, 353). אֵפֶר is the predicate nominative of יִהְיוּ. The implied subject of the verb is רְשָׁעִים of the previous clause.

תַּחַת כַּפּוֹת רַגְלֵיכֶם. Prep + noun f pl constr + noun f dual constr with 2 m pl pronominal suf. The prepositional, genitival phrase modifies אֵפֶר. This phrase is also found in 1 Kgs 5:17.

בַּיּוֹם אֲשֶׁר אֲנִי עֹשֶׂה. בְּ prep with def art and noun m s + rel pron + indep pers pron 1 c s + Qal act ptc m s abs √עָשָׂה. The phrase is similar to that in 3:17. The בְּ preposition functions in a temporal sense as "when" (WO §11.2.5c). For בַּיּוֹם, see note on לְיוֹם in 3:17. The relative pronoun introduces a clause modifying בַּיּוֹם. The first common singular pronoun functions as the subject of עָשָׂה. The participle functions as an intransitive verb and is translated in present tense (WO §37.6e), but given an impending future sense by the future tense discourse of the previous verses. The verb עָשָׂה has the same meaning of "act," as in 3:17 (see verse 17).

אָמַר יְהוָה צְבָאוֹת:. Prophetic messenger formula effectively concluding the sixth oracle.

Appendices (3:22-24)

The last three verses begin the appendices to the book of Malachi. In this section, Yahweh speaks in first person through the prophet. The prophet does not use the prophetic disputation genre so common throughout the book, but rather uses prophetic monologue. These verses have two themes: the law (22) and prophecy (23-24). The writer uses opposites (fathers and sons), as in earlier sections. Like much of Malachi, this section is full of covenant language. Also, this section emphasizes the coming "day of the Lord." Note that some LXX texts have these verses reordered as 23-24, 22 rather than as the Masoretic Text has them ordered (*BHS* note 22ª; see Hill, 363–66; Merrill, 385–86, 451). Most scholars believe 3:22-24 are later additions to the text, serving either to sum up the book of Malachi, the Book of the Twelve, or the Hebrew Bible (see ICC, 4; Hill, 363–66).

Key Words				
אֵלֶיהָ	זָכַר	יוֹם יְהוָה	שׁוּב	תּוֹרַת מֹשֶׁה

Malachi 3:22

²²*"Remember the law of Moses my servant, statutes and judgments which I commanded him at Horeb for all Israel."*

3:22 זִכְרוּ תּוֹרַת מֹשֶׁה עַבְדִּי אֲשֶׁר צִוִּיתִי אוֹתוֹ בְחֹרֵב
עַל־כָּל־יִשְׂרָאֵל חֻקִּים וּמִשְׁפָּטִים:

Verse 22 is a command from Yahweh. The LXX places this verse at
the end of the book (*BHS*, note 22ᵃ). Stuart suggests that the reason
is to end the book on a positive note or to end with an emphasis on
Torah (Stuart, 1392; Merrill, 385–86). *BHS* also suggests this verse
is a later addition to the book (*BHS*, note 22ᵃ). However, verse 22 is
a fitting conclusion, a reemphasis, in that Malachi had addressed the
priests' lack of keeping the law throughout much of the book and specifically in 2:7-8. Furthermore, some scholars see this verse as the last
authentic verse of Malachi (see Verhoef, 337, note 1).

זִכְרוּ תּוֹרַת מֹשֶׁה עַבְדִּי. Qal impv 2 m pl √זָכַר + noun f s
constr + pr noun + noun m s constr with 1 c s pronominal suf. The
verb זִכְרוּ means more than simply "remember" but includes the idea
of "obey" (*NIDOT*, 1:1103). Such remembrance leads to obedience
according to Ps 103:18. The imperative form emphasizes the importance of doing the action. תּוֹרַת מֹשֶׁה is a genitival phrase that is the
object of זִכְרוּ. עַבְדִּי is a modifier of מֹשֶׁה. תּוֹרַת מֹשֶׁה occurs only
here in Malachi and only seven times in the Hebrew Bible (Josh 8:31,
32; 23:6; 2 Kgs 14:6; 23:25; and Neh 8:1). This phrase leaves no doubt
to that the writer is referring to the Sinai covenant, a major theme in
Malachi. For a discussion on תּוֹרָה, see 2:8.

אֲשֶׁר צִוִּיתִי אוֹתוֹ בְחֹרֵב עַל־כָּל־יִשְׂרָאֵל. Subordinate
clause modifying תּוֹרַת מֹשֶׁה introduced by the relative pronoun
אֲשֶׁר.

אֲשֶׁר צִוִּיתִי אוֹתוֹ. Rel pron + Pi *qatal* 1 c s √צָוָה + sign of dir obj
with 3 m s pronominal suf.

בְחֹרֵב עַל־כָּל־יִשְׂרָאֵל. בְּ prep with pr noun + prep – noun m
s constr – pr noun. The בְּ preposition has the spatial sense of location
(WO §11.2.5b). חֹרֵב is a place name synonymous with Sinai for "the
mountain of God" but it does not occur in the prophets except here.
חֹרֵב occurs mostly in Deuteronomy. עַל־כָּל־יִשְׂרָאֵל is a commonly
used phrase that is inclusive of or representative of all the people of
the nation Israel, regardless of whether or not they were present at
Horeb (Stuart, 1391–92). The phrase includes all of the covenant

community, past and present (GM, 251). The preposition עַל when used with a verb of speaking, in this case צִוִּיתִי, takes on the meaning of "concerning" (WO §11.2.13g).

חֻקִּים וּמִשְׁפָּטִים: Noun m pl + *waw* cop with noun m pl. These nouns are parallel terms and are descriptive of תּוֹרַת מֹשֶׁה.

Malachi 3:23-24

²³"Behold I am sending to you Elijah the prophet before the coming day of Yahweh—the great and the terrible. ²⁴And he will cause the hearts of fathers to turn against sons and the hearts of sons to turn against fathers lest I come and I strike the land [with] destruction."

3:23 הִנֵּה אָנֹכִי שֹׁלֵחַ לָכֶם אֵת אֵלִיָּה הַנָּבִיא לִפְנֵי בּוֹא
יוֹם יְהוָה הַגָּדוֹל וְהַנּוֹרָא:

Verses 23 and 24 are independent of the previous verse in context and meaning.

הִנֵּה אָנֹכִי שֹׁלֵחַ לָכֶם אֵת אֵלִיָּה הַנָּבִיא. Independent, declarative clause of pending action.

הִנֵּה אָנֹכִי שֹׁלֵחַ לָכֶם. Demons part (interj) + indep pers pron 1 c s + Qal act ptc m s abs √שָׁלַח + לְ prep with 2 m pl pronominal suf. הִנֵּה is a exclamation of immediacy frequently occurring with pronouns and participles. When הִנֵּה is coupled with a participle, the participle usually functions as a verb with the sense of an impending action in the immediate future (see WO §40.2.1b and GKC §116p). Hill says it is a type of messenger formula that anticipates a speech (Hill, 375–76). The personal pronoun אָנֹכִי functions as the subject of the clause. Hill points out that the use of אָנֹכִי here, the longer form of the first person singular pronoun, is unusual for Malachi. The writer consistently uses אֲנִי in other passages—1:4, 6, 14; 2:9; 3:6, 17, and 21 (Hill, 375; see GM, 252 and see Chart 1 in Appendix). This may be an indication that the verse is a later addition. לָכֶם functions as the indirect object of שָׁלַח. The לְ preposition marks the indirect object (WO §11.2.10d).

אֵת אֵלִיָּה הַנָּבִיא. Sign of dir obj + pr noun + def art with noun m s. הַנָּבִיא modifies אֵלִיָּה. אֵלִיָּה is the personal name "Elijah." The form used here is a shortened form of אֵלִיָּהוּ found in the Elijah cycles. However, it does occur in this form in 1 Kgs 1:3, 4, 8, 12 and in 1 Chron 8:27. הַנָּבִיא is a title for Elijah. The LXX omits this title and adds τὸν Θεσβίτην "the Tishbite," perhaps to conform to the usage of this title in 1 Kgs 17:1; 21:17, 28; 2 Kgs 1:3, 8; and 9:16. Verhoef connects "Elijah the prophet" with "the messenger" of 3:1 (Verhoef, 340); but this is a tenuous connection. Elijah is mentioned frequently in post-Hebrew Bible literature as the forerunner of the Messiah (*NIDOT*, 4:577; Joynes, 577–78). He is mentioned as a person who had a burning zeal for the law and for this reason he was taken into heaven, according to 1 Macc 2:58. This association between Elijah, the law, and his return is implied here. Sirach 48:1-11 uses similar language to that of Malachi but greatly expands upon it. In addition to associating Elijah with the "day of the Lord," Sirach includes "turning back the hearts of toward their sons" and then adds "and to reestablish the tribes of Jacob" (Sir 28:10, New American Bible, rev. ed.; see Joynes, 577). The New Testament associates John the Baptist with Elijah as the forerunner of the Messiah (Matt 11:14; Luke 1:17; and others). Luke 1:17 has similar wording as Mal 3:24.

לִפְנֵי בּוֹא יוֹם יְהוָה הַגָּדוֹל וְהַנּוֹרָא. Subordinate clause.

לִפְנֵי בּוֹא. Prep + Qal inf constr √בּוֹא. On the preposition, see note on לִפְנֵי in 3:1. The combination of the verb בּוֹא with יוֹם is reflective of the usage of these words in 3:1 and 2.

יוֹם יְהוָה. Noun m s constr + pr noun. This is a construct genitive phrase and is very common in prophetic literature (frequently used in Isaiah, Joel, and Amos) expressing Yahweh's impending judgment that is to come. See notes on יוֹם in 3:17 and 19.

הַגָּדוֹל וְהַנּוֹרָא. Def art with adj m s + *waw* cop with def art and Ni ptc m s abs √יָרֵא. The Niphal participle functions as an adjective. These adjectives are in apposition to יוֹם יְהוָה and refer to the quality or character of the day (WO §12.3c).

3:24 וְהֵשִׁיב לֵב־אָבוֹת עַל־בָּנִים וְלֵב בָּנִים עַל־אֲבוֹתָם פֶּן־ אָבוֹא וְהִכֵּיתִי אֶת־הָאָרֶץ חֵרֶם:

וְהֵשִׁיב לֵב־אָבוֹת עַל־בָּנִים. Hi *weqatal* 3 m s √שׁוּב + noun m s constr – noun m pl + prep – noun m pl. The *waw* is conjunctive, joining this clause with the previous one. Furthermore, the *weqatal* form continues the future tense. The Hiphil form of שׁוּב has the meaning of "bring back" or "restore" (Stuart, 1395). See discussion on שׁוּב in 3:7. The subject of הֵשִׁיב is אֵלִיָּה from the previous verse. The preposition עַל can have the sense of "against" (WO §11.2.13f); however, the preposition can have a joining function with the terminative sense when used in conjunction with verbs of motion and is translated "to" (WO §11.2.13b), as the context suggests here.

וְלֵב בָּנִים עַל־אֲבוֹתָם. *Waw* cop with noun m s constr + noun m pl + prep – noun m pl constr with 3 m pl pronominal suf. This phrase is a redirection of the previous phrase, indicating the completeness of the restorative (שׁוּב) task of Elijah. The preposition עַל functions here the same as in the phrase above.

פֶּן־אָבוֹא וְהִכֵּיתִי אֶת־הָאָרֶץ חֵרֶם: Dependent clause expressing result, if the conditions of the previous clause are not met.

פֶּן־אָבוֹא. Conj – Qal *yiqtol* 1 c s √בוֹא. The conjunction פֶּן expresses the mood of contingency (WO §31.6.1b). The *yiqtol* verb has a model sense, that the future action is uncertain but may happen (MNK, 168–69).

וְהִכֵּיתִי. Hi *weqatal* 1 c s √נָכָה. This verb occurs almost exclusively in the Hiphil and does not have a causative sense.

אֶת־הָאָרֶץ חֵרֶם׃. Sign of dir obj – def art with noun m s + noun m s. The phrase is a double accusative and functions as the direct object and means (WO §10.2.3d). In such cases, the English preposition "with" must be added between the nouns for coherence. חֵרֶם connotes divine judgment which results in destruction (*NIDOT*, 2:260–61).

CHART 1

Hebrew Words Occurring in Malachi

Hebrew Word	Word Form	Occurrences
אָב	noun	1:6 [2x]; 2:10 [2x]; 3:7, 24 [2x]
אֱדוֹם	proper noun	1:4
אָדָם	noun	3:8
אֲדָמָה	noun	3:11
אָדוֹן	noun	1:6 [2x], 12, 14; 3:1
אָהַב	verb	1:2 [3x]; 2:11
אֹהֶל	noun	2:12
אוֹ	conjunction	1:8; 2:17
אוֹר	verb	1:10
אָז	adverb	3:16
אָח	noun	1:2; 2:10
אֶחָד	numeral	2:10 [2x], 15 [2x]
אַיֵּה	interrogative	1:6 [2x]; 2:17
אַיִן	negative substantive	1:8 [2x], 10; 2:2, 9, 13

Hebrew Word	Word Form	Occurrences
אִישׁ	noun	2:10, 12; 3:16, 17
אֹכֶל	noun	1:12; 3:11
אֵל	noun	1:9; 2:10, 11
אֶל	preposition	1:1, 2:1, 3, 4, 13; 3:1, 5, 7 [2x], 10
אַל	negative	2:15
אֱלֹהִים	noun	2:15, 16, 17; 3:8, 14, 15, 18
אֵלִיָּה	proper noun	3:23
אַלְמָנָה	noun	3:5
אִם	hypothetical particle	1:6 [2x]; 2:2 [2x]; 3:10
אָמַר	verb	1:2 [2x], 4 [2x], 5, 6 [2x], 7 [2x], 8, 9, 10, 11, 12, 13 [3x], 14; 2:2, 4, 8, 14, 16 [2x], 17; 3:1, 5, 7 [2x], 8, 10, 11, 12, 13 [2x], 14, 17, 19, 21
אֱמֶת	noun	2:6
אֲנִי	independent personal pronoun	1:4, 6 [2x], 14; 2:9; 3:6, 17, 21
אֲנַחְנוּ	independent personal pronoun	3:15
אָנֹכִי	independent personal pronoun	3:23
אֲנָקָה	noun	2:13
אֵפֶר	noun	3:21
אוֹצָר	noun	3:10
אֲרֻבָּה	noun	3:10
אֶרֶץ	noun	3:12, 24

Chart 1   123

Hebrew Word	Word Form	Occurrences
אָרַר	verb	1:14; 2:2 [2x]; 3:9
אֵשׁ	noun	3:2
אִשָּׁה	noun	2:14 [2x], 15
אָשַׁר	verb	3:12, 15
אֲשֶׁר	relative particle	1:4; 2:9, 11, 12, 14; 3:1 [2x], 17, 18, 19, 21, 22
אֵת	sign of direct object	1:2 [2x], 3 [2x], 6, 12, 13 [5x]; 2:2 [2x], 3 [3x], 4 [2x], 5, 9, 13; 3:2, 3 [2x], 8, 9, 10 [2x], 11, 12, 16, 17, 19, 22, 23, 24
אֵת	preposition	2:6
אַתָּה	independent personal pronoun	2:14
אַתֶּם	independent personal pronoun	1:5, 12; 2:8; 3:1 [2x], 6, 8, 9 [2x], 12
בָּגַד	verb	2:10, 11, 14, 15, 16
בּוֹא	verb	1:13 [2x]; 3:1 [2x], 2, 10, 19 [2x], 23, 24
בָּזָה	verb	1:6 [2x], 7, 12; 2:9
בָּחַן	verb	3:10, 15
בֵּין	preposition	2:14 [2x]; 3:18 [2x]
בַּיִת	noun	3:10 [2x]
בְּכִי	noun	2:13
בְּלִי	noun	3:10
בֵּן	noun	1:6; 3:3, 6, 17, 24 [2x]
בָּנָה	verb	1:4 [2x]; 3:15
בָּעַל	verb	2:11

Hebrew Word	Word Form	Occurrences
בָּעַר	noun	3:19
בֶּצַע	noun	3:14
בָּקַשׁ	verb	2:7, 15; 3:1
בָּרָא	verb	2:10.
בְּרִית	noun	2:4, 5, 8, 10, 14; 3:1, 2
בְּרָכָה	noun	2:2; 3:10
בַּת	noun	2:11
גָּאַל	verb	1:7 [2x], 12
גְּבוּל	noun	1:4, 5
גָּדַל	verb	1:5
גָּדוֹל	adjective	1:11 [2x], 14; 3:23
גּוֹי	noun	1:11 [2x], 14; 3:9, 12
גָּזַל	verb	1:13
גַּם	conjunction	1:10; 2:2, 9; 3:15 [2x]
גָּעַר	verb	2:3; 3:11
גֶּפֶן	noun	3:11
גֵּר	noun	3:5
דָּבַר	verb	3:16
דָּבָר	noun	1:1; 2:17; 3:13
דַּי	noun	3:10
דֶּלֶת	noun	1:10
דִּמְעָה	noun	2:13

Chart 1   125

Hebrew Word	Word Form	Occurrences
דַּעַת	noun	2:7
דֶּרֶךְ	noun	2:8, 9; 3:1
הוּא	independent personal pronoun	1:7, 12; 2:5, 7, 17; 3:2
הִיא	independent personal pronoun	2:14
הָיָה	verb	1:9; 2:4, 5, 6; 3:3, 5, 10, 12, 17, 19, 21
הֵיכָל	noun	3:1
הָלַךְ	*verb*	2:6; 3:14
הֵמָּה	independent personal pronoun	1:4
הִנֵּה	interjection	1:13; 2:3; 3:1 [2x], 19, 23
הִנָּם	adverb	1:10
הַר	noun	1:3
הָרַס	verb	1:4
זֹאת	demon-strative or relative pronoun	1:9; 2:1, 4, 13; 3:10
זָבַח	verb	1:8, 14
זֵד	adjective	3:15, 19
זָהָב	noun	3:3
זָכַר	verb	3:22
זָכָר	noun	1:14
זִכָּרוֹן	noun	3:16

Hebrew Word	Word Form	Occurrences
זָעַם	verb	1:4
זָקַק	verb	3:3
זָרָה	verb	2:3
זָרַח	verb	3:20
זֶרַע	noun	2:3, 15
חֲבֶרֶת	noun	2:14
חַג	noun	2:3
חָזַק	verb	3:13
חַי	noun	2:5
חָלָה	verb	1:8, 9, 13
חָלַל	verb	1:12; 2:10, 11
חָמַל	verb	3:17 [2x]
חָמַס	verb	2:16
חָנַן	verb	1:9
חָפֵץ	verb	2:17
חֵפֶץ	noun	1:10; 3:12
חָפֵץ	adjective	3:1
חֹק	noun	3:7, 22
חֹרֵב	proper noun	3:22
חָרְבָּה	noun	1:4
חֵרֶם	noun	3:24
חָשַׁב	verb	3:16

Chart 1   127

Hebrew Word	Word Form	Occurrences
חָתַת	verb	2:5
טָהֵר	verb	3:3 [2x]
טָהוֹר	adjective	1:11
טוֹב	adjective	2:17
יָגַע	verb	2:17 [2x]
יָד	noun	1:1, 9, 10, 13; 2:13
יָדַע	verb	2:4
יהוה	divine name; proper noun	1:1, 2 [2x], 4 [2x], 5, 6, 7, 8, 9, 10, 11, 13 [2x], 14; 2:2, 4, 7, 8, 11, 12 [2x], 13, 14, 16 [2x], 17 [2x]; 3:1, 3, 4, 5, 6, 7, 10, 11, 12, 13, 14, 16 [3x], 17, 19, 21, 23
יְהוּדָה	proper noun	2:11 [2x]; 3:4
יוֹם	noun	3:2, 4, 7, 17, 19 [2x], 21, 23
יָמִים	noun	3:5
יַעֲקֹב	proper noun	1:2 [2x]; 2:12; 3:6
יָצָא	verb	3:20
יָרֵא	verb	1:14; 2:5; 3:5, 16 [2x], 20, 23
יְרוּשָׁלַם	proper noun	2:11; 3:4
יִשְׂרָאֵל	proper noun	1:1, 5; 2:11, 16; 3:22
יֵשׁ	adverb	1:14
יָשַׁב	verb	3:3
כַּאֲשֶׁר	relative particle	3:17
כָּבֵד	verb	1:6
כָּבוֹד	noun	1:6; 2:2

Hebrew Word	Word Form	Occurrences
כָּבַס	verb	3:2
כֹּה	demonstrative adverb	1:4
כֹּהֵן	noun	1:6; 2:1, 7
כּוּל	verb	3:2
כִּי	conjunction	1:4, 8 [2x], 11 [2x], 14; 2:2, 4, 7 [2x], 11, 14, 16; 3:2, 6, 8, 12, 14 [2x], 19, 21
כֹּל	noun	1:11; 2:9, 10, 17; 3:9, 10, 12, 19 [2x], 22
כָּלָה	verb	3:6
כָּנָף	noun	3:20
כָּסָה	verb	2:13, 16
כֶּסֶף	noun	3:3 [2x]
כַּף	noun	3:21
כָּרַת	verb	2:12
כָּשַׁל	verb	2:8
כָּשַׁף	verb	3:5
כָּתַב	verb	3:16
לֵב	noun	2:2 [2x]; 3:24 [2x]
לְבוּשׁ	noun	2:16
לָהַט	verb	3:19
לֹא	negative	1:2, 10 [2x]; 2:2 [2x], 6, 10 [2x], 15, 16; 3:5, 6 [2x], 7, 10, 11 [2x], 18, 19
לֵוִי	noun	2:4, 8; 3:3
לֶחֶם	noun	1:7
לִפְנֵי	preposition	3:1, 16, 23

Chart 1 129

Hebrew Word	Word Form	Occurrences
לָקַח	verb	2:13
מְאֵרָה	noun	2:2; 3:9
מָבוֹא	noun	1:11
מִדְבָּר	noun	1:3
מַדּוּעַ	noun	2:10
מָה	interrogative	1:2, 6, 7; 2:14, 15, 17; 3:7, 8, 13, 14
מָהַר	verb	3:5
מוֹרָא	noun	1:6; 2:5
מִזְבֵּחַ	noun	1:7, 10; 2:13
מִזְרָח	noun	1:11
מִי	interrogative	1:10; 3:2 [2x]
מִישׁוֹר	noun	2:6
מַלְאָךְ	noun	1:1; 3:1 [2x], 7
מָלַט	verb	3:15
מֶלֶךְ	noun	1:14
מִנְחָה	noun	1:10, 11, 13; 2:12, 13; 3:3, 4
מַעֲשֵׂר	noun	3:8, 10
מָצָא	verb	2:6
מִצְוָה	noun	2:1, 4
מָקוֹם	noun	1:11
מֻקְטָר	noun	1:11
מַרְבֵּק	noun	3:20

Hebrew Word	Word Form	Occurrences
מַרְפֵּא	noun	3:20
מַשָּׂא	noun	1:1
מֹשֶׁה	noun	3:22
מִשְׁמֶרֶת	noun	3:14
מִשְׁפָּט	noun	2:17; 3:5, 22
נָא	particle of entreaty	1:8, 9; 3:10
נְאֻם	noun	1:2
נָאַף	verb	3:5
נָבִיא	noun	3:23
נָגַשׁ	verb	1:7, 8 [2x], 11; 2:12; 3:3
נָדַר	verb	1:14
נַחֲלָה	noun	1:3
נָטָה	verb	3:5
נִיב	noun	1:12
נָכָה	verb	3:24
נָכַל	verb	1:14
נֵכָר	noun	2:11
נַעַר	noun	2:14, 15
נָפַח	verb	1:13
נָשָׂא	verb	1:8, 9; 2:3, 9
נָתַן	verb	2:2, 5, 9
סְגֻלָּה	noun	3:17

Chart 1   131

Hebrew Word	Word Form	Occurrences
סָגַר	verb	1:10
סוּר	verb	2:8; 3:7
סֵפֶר	noun	3:16
עָבַד	verb	3:14, 17, 18 [2x]
עֶבֶד	noun	1:6; 3:22
עֵגֶל	noun	3:20
עַד	preposition	1:4, 11; 3:10
עֵד	noun	3:5
עֵדֶר	noun	1:14
עוּד	verb	2:14
עוֹד	adverb	2:13
עוֹלָה	noun	2:6
עוֹלָם	noun	1:4; 3:4
עָוֹן	noun	2:6
עִוֵּר	adjective	1:8
עָזַב	verb	3:19
עַיִן	noun	1:5; 2:17
עַל	preposition	1:5, 7; 2:2 [2x], 3, 14 [2x], 16; 3:13 [2x], 17 [2x], 22, 24 [2x]
עַם	noun	1:4; 2:9
עָמַד	verb	3:2
עָנָה	verb	2:12
עָנָף	noun	3:19

Hebrew Word	Word Form	Occurrences
עָסַס	verb	3:21
עַר	noun	2:12
עָרַב	verb	3:4
עָשָׂה	verb	2:11, 12, 13, 15, 17; 3:15, 17, 19, 21
עֵשָׂו	proper noun	1:2, 3
עָשַׁק	verb	3:5
עַתָּה	adverb	1:9; 2:1; 3:15
פֶּה	noun	2:6, 7, 9
פּוּשׁ	verb	3:20
פֶּחָה	noun	1:8
פֶּן	conjunction	3:24
פָּנֶה	noun	1:8, 9 [2x]; 2:3, 5, 9, 13; 3:1, 14
פִּסֵּחַ	adjective	1:8, 13
פְּרִי	noun	3:11
פֶּרֶשׁ	noun	2:3 [2x]
פִּתְאֹם	noun	3:1
פָּתָה	verb	3:10
צְבָאוֹת	noun	1:4, 6, 8, 9, 10, 11, 13, 14; 2:2, 4, 7, 8, 12, 16; 3:1, 5, 7, 10, 11, 12, 14, 17, 19, 21
צַדִּיק	noun	3:18
צְדָקָה	noun	3:3, 20
צָוָה	verb	3:22
צָרַף	verb	3:2, 3

Chart 1   133

Hebrew Word	Word Form	Occurrences
קָבַע	verb	3:8 [3x], 9
קַדְמֹנִי	adjective	3:4
קִדֹרַנִּית	adjective	3:14
קֹדֶשׁ	noun	2:11
קָרָא	verb	1:4
קָרַב	verb	1:8; 3:5
קַשׁ	noun	3:19
קָשַׁב	verb	3:16
רָאָה	verb	1:5; 3:2, 18
רַב	noun	2:6, 8
רֶגֶל	noun	3:21
רוּחַ	noun	2:15 [2x], 16
רִיק	verb	3:10
רֵעַ	noun	3:16
רַע	adjective	1:8 [2x]; 2:17
רָצָה	verb	1:8, 10, 13
רָצוֹן	noun	2:13
רָשַׁע	verb	3:18, 21
רִשְׁעָה	noun	1:4; 3:15, 19
רָשַׁשׁ	verb	1:4
שָׂדֶה	noun	3:11
שִׂים	verb	1:3; 2:2 [2x]

Hebrew Word	Word Form	Occurrences
שָׂכִיר	noun	3:5
שָׂכָר	noun	3:5
שָׂנֵא	verb	1:3; 2:16
שָׂפָה	verb	2:6, 7
שְׁאָר	noun	2:15
שָׁבַע	verb	3:5
שָׁוְא	noun	3:14
שׁוּב	verb	1:4; 2:6; 3:7 [3x], 18, 24
שָׁחַת	verb	1:14; 2:8; 3:11
שָׁכַל	verb	3:11
שָׁלוֹם	noun	2:5, 6
שָׁלַח	verb	2:2, 4, 16; 3:1, 23
שֻׁלְחָן	noun	1:7, 12
שֵׁם	noun	1:6 [2x], 11 [3x], 14; 2:2, 5; 3:16, 20
שָׁמַיִם	noun	3:10
שְׁמָמָה	noun	1:3
שָׁמַע	verb	2:2; 3:16
שָׁמַר	verb	2:7, 9, 15, 16; 3:7, 14
שֶׁמֶשׁ	noun	1:11; 3:20
שֵׁנִי	numeral	2:13
שָׁנָה	verb	3:6
שָׁנָה	noun	3:4

Chart 1 135

Hebrew Word	Word Form	Occurrences
שָׁפָל	adjective	2:9
שֶׁקֶר	noun	3:5
שֹׁרֶשׁ	noun	3:19
תּוֹעֵבָה	noun	2:11
תּוֹרָה	noun	2:6, 7, 8, 9; 3:22
תַּחַת	preposition	3:21
תְּלָאָה	noun	1:13
תַּן	noun	1:3
תַּנּוּר	noun	3:19
תְּרוּמָה	noun	3:8

CHART 2

Occurrences of the Divine Messenger Formula in Malachi

Messenger Formula or Similar Phrasing	Location
אָמַר יְהוָה	1:2
נְאֻם יְהוָה	1:2
אָמַר יְהוָה צְבָאוֹת	1:4
אָמַר יְהוָה צְבָאוֹת לָכֶם	1:6
אָמַר יְהוָה צְבָאוֹת	1:8
אָמַר יְהוָה צְבָאוֹת	1:9
אָמַר יְהוָה צְבָאוֹת	1:10
אָמַר יְהוָה צְבָאוֹת	1:11
אָמַר יְהוָה צְבָאוֹת	1:13
אָמַר יְהוָה	1:13
אָמַר יְהוָה צְבָאוֹת	1:14
אָמַר יְהוָה צְבָאוֹת	2:2
אָמַר יְהוָה צְבָאוֹת	2:4
יְהוָה צְבָאוֹת הוּא	2:7
אָמַר יְהוָה צְבָאוֹת	2:8
לַיהוָה צְבָאוֹת	2:12

Chart 2 137

Messenger Formula or Similar Phrasing	Location
אָמַר יְהוָה אֱלֹהֵי יִשְׂרָאֵל	2:16
אָמַר יְהוָה צְבָאוֹת	2:16
אָמַר יְהוָה צְבָאוֹת	3:1
אָמַר יְהוָה צְבָאוֹת	3:5
אָמַר יְהוָה צְבָאוֹת	3:7
אָמַר יְהוָה צְבָאוֹת	3:10
אָמַר יְהוָה צְבָאוֹת	3:11
אָמַר יְהוָה צְבָאוֹת	3:12
אָמַר יְהוָה	3:13
יְהוָה צְבָאוֹת	3:14
אָמַר יְהוָה צְבָאוֹת	3:17
אָמַר יְהוָה צְבָאוֹת	3:19
אָמַר יְהוָה צְבָאוֹת	3:21

GLOSSARY

ablative—a case that marks movement away from something.

adversative—a word or phrase that expresses opposition or antithesis.

allative—a form that has the spatial sense of moving toward.

anacoenosis—an appeal to others based upon a common interest.

apodosis—a conditional clause expressing result or consequences.

appellation—word, phrase, or name that describes or identifies a person or thing.

apposition—the placement of two nouns or noun phrases in juxtaposition, with one noun serving as a descriptive or explanatory modifier of the other, with both having the same syntactic function.

auxiliary—a verb, in a subordinate position, that assists another verb in expressing tense, mood, or some aspect of the primary verb.

chiasm—a literary device in which syntactical elements cross. The latter elements form a mirror image of the former elements thus resembling the Greek letter *chi* (X).

clause—a group of words with a subject and only one predicate, which may or may not have a verb.

collective singular—a singular noun functioning as a plural.

direct object—the noun that receives the action of a transitive verb.

disjunctive—a conjunction or word that establishes a contrast between words or clauses.

dittography—an accidental duplication of a letter in the copying or in the writing of a text.

double entendre—a term having two meanings.

enveloping—grammatical structure that frames a pericope, indicating its opening and closing as well as signifying the pericope's unity.

epexegesis—an additional explanation of the previous clause or statement.

fronting—the placement of a subject or object before a verbal form with the result of focus upon the item fronted.

gapping—a condition where a verb is intentionally omitted from the second clause of parallel clauses with the identical notion of the verb carrying over from the first clause into the second without restating it.

genitive—a relationship between nouns denoting attribute or possession, but can indicate additional relationships.

hapax legomenon—a word or form occurring only once in the Hebrew Bible.

hortatory—a word, clause, or sentence of direct dialogue.

hyperbole—intentional exaggeration or overstatement for effect.

indirect object—a noun that receives the direct object in a clause.

interjection—an exclamation placed between words or phrases that have no grammatical connection.

interrogative—a word or particle that introduces a question.

intransitive verb—a verb that does not require a direct object.

jussive—a volitional expression that conveys a wish or indirect command in the *yiqtol* third or second person. In weak verbs, the jussive may appear apocopated (shortened).

logical marker—a conjunction, particle, or grammatical marker that indicates the next part of a sequence.

merismus—a poetic device in which an idea is alluded to by reference to its two parts, often expressed in opposite terms.

metaphor—a comparison of one thing to another, usually without the comparative "as" or "like."

nonperfective—a condition where the structure of the movement or condition is over time and is not specified, inferring a continuing or ongoing state.

parallelism—a syntactical structure where elements parallel each other in some manner. The second member completes the first member by restatement, contrast, or amplification.

pejorative—a word, phrase, or clause with a disparaging or derogatory meaning.

periphrastic—use of many words in the place of one or a few.

predicate adjective—a word following a linking verb that modifies the subject of the clause.

predicate nominative—a noun following a linking verb that restates or stands in for the subject.

progressive—a term for tenses denoting a continuing state for the *yiqtol* form. For example, in English, it is rendered "he is eating."

protasis—introductory clause stating a condition; the "if" part of an "if"–"then" statement.

pseudo-dialogue—a hypothetical conversation between parties given in dialogue format.

simile—comparison of two unlike things, usually using the qualifier "like" or "as."

spatial—an expression describing how a noun relates to space.

stative verb—a verb or verb form describing a state or quality rather than an action.

subordinate clause—any clause that stands in relationship to an independent clause. Also referred to as a dependent clause.

substantive—a word functioning as a noun which names things or beings.

superlative—highest degree of an adjective, usually translated in English with the ending "est."

syntax—the study of clauses and sentences in a language, in which particular attention is given to the formal connections and relationships that exist between the elements found therein.

transitive verb—a verb that requires a direct object.

vocative—a grammatical case marking direct address.

***waw* copulative**—the normal conjunction that is prefixed to any word to connect words, phrases, or clauses. Also known as the "*waw* conjunction." The *waw* copulative has no semantic value, other than that of "and."

BIBLIOGRAPHY

Allen, Leslie C. "זכר." Pages 1100–1106 in vol. 1 of *New International Dictionary of Old Testament Theology and Exegesis*. Edited by Willem A. VanGemeren. 5 vols. Grand Rapids: Zondervan, 1997.

Arnold, Bill T., and John H. Choi. *A Guide to Biblical Hebrew Syntax*. Cambridge: Cambridge University Press, 2003.

Averbeck, Richard E. "גָּאַל." Pages 794–95 in vol. 1 of *New International Dictionary of Old Testament Theology and Exegesis*. Edited by Willem A. VanGemeren. 5 vols. Grand Rapids: Zondervan, 1997.

———. "מִנְחָה." Pages 978–90 in vol. 2 of *New International Dictionary of Old Testament Theology and Exegesis*. Edited by Willem A. VanGemeren. 5 vols. Grand Rapids: Zondervan, 1997.

———. "תְּרוּמָה." Pages 335–38 in vol. 4 of *New International Dictionary of Old Testament Theology and Exegesis*. Edited by Willem A. VanGemeren. 5 vols. Grand Rapids: Zondervan, 1997.

———. "מַעֲשֵׂר." Pages 1035–55 in vol. 2 of *New International Dictionary of Old Testament Theology and Exegesis*. Edited by Willem A. VanGemeren. 5 vols. Grand Rapids: Zondervan, 1997.

Baker, David W. "רעע." Pages 1154–58 in vol. 3 of *New International Dictionary of Old Testament Theology and Exegesis*. Edited by Willem A. VanGemeren. 5 vols. Grand Rapids: Zondervan, 1997.

Baldwin, Joyce G. *Haggai, Zechariah, Malachi: An Introduction and Commentary*. Downers Grove, Ill: InterVarsity, 1972.

Bernhardt, K. H. "הָיָה." Pages 372–75 in vol. 3 of *Theological Dictionary of the Old Testament*. Edited by G. Johannes Botterweck and Helmer Ringgren. Translated by John T. Willis and Geoffrey W. Bromiley. 15 vols. Grand Rapids: Eerdmans, 1978.

Berry, Donald K. "Malachi's Dual Design: The Close of the Canon and What Comes Afterward." Pages 269–302 in *Forming Prophetic Literature: Essays on Isaiah and the Twelve in Honor of John D. W. Watts*. Edited by James W. Watts and Paul R. House. Journal for the Study of the Old Testament Supplement Series 235. Sheffield: Sheffield Academic, 1996.

Brensinger, Terry L. "בחן." Pages 636–38 in vol. 1 of *New International Dictionary of Old Testament Theology and Exegesis*. Edited by Willem A. VanGemeren. 5 vols. Grand Rapids: Zondervan, 1997.

Brenton, Sir Lancelot C. L. *The Septuagint with Apocrypha: Greek and English*. London: Samuel Bagster & Sons, 1851. Repr. Peabody, Mass.: Hendrickson, 1985.

Brown, Francis I., with S. R. Driver, and Charles A. Briggs. *A Hebrew and English Lexicon of the Old Testament*. Oxford: Clarendon, 1907.

Brown, Michael L. "ברך." Pages 757–67 in vol. 1 of *New International Dictionary of Old Testament Theology and Theology and Exegesis*. Edited by Willem A. VanGemeren. 5 vols. Grand Rapids: Zondervan, 1997.

Buth, Randall. "Word Order in the Verbless Clause: A Generative-Functional Approach." Pages 79–108 in *The Verbless Clause in Biblical Hebrew: Linguistic Approaches*. Edited by Cynthia L. Miller. Linguistic Studies in Ancient West Semitic 1. Winona Lake, Ind.: Eisenbrauns, 1999.

Caquot, A. "גער." Pages 49–53 in vol. 3 of *Theological Dictionary of the Old Testament*. Edited by G. Johannes Botterweck and Helmer Ringgren. Translated by John T. Willis, Geoffrey W. Bromiley, and David E. Green. 15 vols. Grand Rapids: Eerdmans, 1977.

Carpenter, Eugene, and Michael A. Grisanti. "רשע." Pages 1201–4 in vol. 3 of *New International Dictionary of Old Testament Theology and Theology and Exegesis*. Edited by Willem A. VanGemeren. 5 vols. Grand Rapids: Zondervan, 1997.

Chisholm, Robert B. "שנה." Pages 190–91 in vol. 4 of *New International Dictionary of Old Testament Theology and Theology and Exegesis*. Edited by Willem A. VanGemeren. 5 vols. Grand Rapids: Zondervan, 1997.

Clements, Ronald E. "גּוֹי." Pages 426–33 in vol. 2 of *Theological Dictionary of the Old Testament*. Rev. ed. Edited by G. Johannes Botterweck and Helmer Ringgren. Translated by John T. Willis. 15 vols. Grand Rapids: Eerdmans, 1977.

Collins, C. John. "כבד." Pages 577–87 in vol. 2 of *New International Dictionary of Old Testament Theology and Theology and Exegesis*. Edited by Willem A. VanGemeren. 5 vols. Grand Rapids: Zondervan, 1997.

Eissfeldt, Otto. *The Old Testament: An Introduction including the Apocrypha and Pseudepigrapha, and also the works of similar type from Qumran*. Translated by Peter R. Ackroyd. New York: Harper & Row, 1965.

Elliger, K., and W. Ruldolf. *Biblica Hebraica Stuttgartensia*. Stuttgart: Deutsche Bibelgesellschaft, 1984.

Els, P. J. J. S. "אָהַב." Pages 277–99 in vol. 1 of *New International Dictionary of Old Testament Theology and Theology and Exegesis*. Edited by Willem A. VanGemeren. 5 vols. Grand Rapids: Zondervan, 1997.

Enns, Peter. "הֶרֶב." Pages 259–62 in vol. 2 of *New International Dictionary of Old Testament Theology and Exegesis*. Edited by Willem A. VanGemeren. 5 vols. Grand Rapids: Zondervan, 1997.

———. "מִשְׁפָּט." Pages 1142–44 in vol. 2 of *New International Dictionary of Old Testament Theology and Exegesis*. Edited by Willem A. VanGemeren. 5 vols. Grand Rapids: Zondervan, 1997.

———. "Law of God." Pages 893–900 in vol. 4 of *New International Dictionary of Old Testament Theology and Exegesis*. Edited by Willem A. VanGemeren. 5 vols. Grand Rapids: Zondervan, 1997.

Fohrer, Georg, and Ernest Sellin. *Introduction to the Old Testament*. Translated by David E. Green. Nashville: Abingdon, 1968.

Fuhs, H. F. "גָּעַל." Pages 45–48 in vol. 3 of *Theological Dictionary of the Old Testament*. Edited by G. Johannes Botterweck and Helmer Ringgren. Translated by John T. Willis and Geoffrey W. Bromiley. 15 vols. Grand Rapids: Eerdmans, 1978.

Glazier-McDonald, Beth. *Malachi: The Divine Messenger*. SBL Dissertation Series 98. Atlanta: Scholars, 1987.

Gordon, Robert P. "ארר." Pages 524–26 in vol. 1 of *New Interna-*

tional Dictionary of Old Testament Theology and Exegesis. Edited by Willem A. VanGemeren. 5 vols. Grand Rapids: Zondervan, 1997.

———. "טוב." Pages 353–57 in vol. 2 of *New International Dictionary of Old Testament Theology and Exegesis*. Edited by Willem A. VanGemeren. 5 vols. Grand Rapids: Zondervan, 1997.

Grisanti, Michael A. "בָּזָה." Pages 628–30 in vol. 1 of *New International Dictionary of Old Testament Theology and Exegesis*. Edited by Willem A. VanGemeren. 5 vols. Grand Rapids: Zondervan, 1997.

———. "תעב." Pages 314–18 in vol. 4 of *New International Dictionary of Old Testament Theology and Exegesis*. Edited by Willem A. VanGemeren. 5 vols. Grand Rapids: Zondervan, 1997.

Hadley, Judith M. "Elijah and Elisha." Pages 572–78 in vol. 4 of *New International Dictionary of Old Testament Theology and Exegesis*. Edited by Willem A. VanGemeren. 5 vols. Grand Rapids: Zondervan, 1997.

Hill, Andrew E. *Malachi*. Anchor Bible 25D. New York: Doubleday, 1998.

Holladay, William L., ed. *A Concise Hebrew and Aramaic Lexicon of the Old Testament*. Grand Rapids: Eerdmans, 1988.

Johnston, Gordon H. "אָדוֹן." Pages 256–61 in vol. 1 of *New International Dictionary of Old Testament Theology and Exegesis*. Edited by Willem A. VanGemeren. 5 vols. Grand Rapids: Zondervan, 1997.

Joynes, Christine E. "Elijah." Pages 577–87 in *The Eerdmans Dictionary of Early Judaism*. Edited by John J. Collins and Daniel C. Harlow. Grand Rapids: Eerdmans, 2010.

Kaiser, Walter C., Jr. *Malachi: God's Unchanging Love*. Grand Rapids: Baker, 1984.

Kautzsch, Emil, ed. *Gesenius' Hebrew Grammar*. Translated and revised by A. E. Cowley. 2nd English ed. Oxford: Clarendon, 1910.

Keil, C. F. "Malachi." In *Commentaty on the Old Testament*. Vol. 10: *Minor Prophets*. Edited by C. F. Keil and F. Delitzsch. Edinburgh: T&T Clark, 1891. Repr. Peabody, Mass.: Hendrickson, 1996.

Kellerman, Diether. "בצע." Pages 205–8 in vol. 2 of *Theological Dictionary of the Old Testament*. Rev. ed. Edited by G. Johannes Botterweck and Helmer Ringgren. Translated by John T. Willis. 15 vols. Grand Rapids: Eerdmans, 1977.

———. "גוּר." Pages 439–49 in vol. 2 of *Theological Dictionary of the Old Testament*. Rev. ed. Edited by G. Johannes Botterweck and Helmer Ringgren. Translated by John T. Willis. 15 vols. Grand Rapids: Eerdmans, 1977.

Kelley, Page H. *Biblical Hebrew: An Introductory Grammar*. Grand Rapids: Eerdmans, 1992.

Koehler, Ludwig, and Walter Baumgartner. *The Hebrew and Aramaic Lexicon of the Old Testament*. 2 vols. Revised by Walter Baumgartner and Johann Jakob Stamm. Translated by M. E. J. Richardson. Leiden: Brill, 2001.

Konkel, A. H. "כֶּסֶף." Pages 683–84 in vol. 2 of *New International Dictionary of Old Testament Theology and Exegesis*. Edited by Willem A. VanGemeren. 5 vols. Grand Rapids: Zondervan, 1997.

———. "שָׂנֵא." Pages 1256–60 in vol. 3 of *New International Dictionary of Old Testament Theology and Exegesis*. Edited by Willem A. VanGemeren. 5 vols. Grand Rapids: Zondervan, 1997.

Lambdin, Thomas O. *Introduction to Biblical Hebrew*. New York: Charles Scribner's Sons, 1971.

Martins, Elmer A. "עָמַד." Pages 432–34 in vol. 3 of *New International Dictionary of Old Testament Theology and Exegesis*. Edited by Willem A. VanGemeren. 5 vols. Grand Rapids: Zondervan, 1997.

McConville, Gordon J. "בְּרִית." Pages 747–55 in vol. 1 of *New International Dictionary of Old Testament Theology and Exegesis*. Edited by Willem A. VanGemeren. 5 vols. Grand Rapids: Zondervan, 1997.

Merrill, Eugene H. *Haggai, Zechariah, Malachi: an Exegetical Commentary*. Chicago: Moody, 1994.

Merwe, Christo H. J. van der, Jackie A. Naudé, and Jan H. Kroeze. *A Biblical Hebrew Reference Grammar*. Biblical Languages: Hebrew 3. New York: Sheffield Academic Press, Continuum, 2006.

Niccacci, Alviero. "Poetic Syntax and Interpretation of Malachi." *Liber Annuus* 51 (2001): 55–107.

O'Brien, Julia M. *Priest and Levite in Malachi*. SBL Dissertation Series 121. Edited by David L. Petersen. Atlanta: Scholars Press, 1990.

Owens, John Joseph. *Analytical Key to the Old Testament*. Vol. 4: *Isaiah–Malachi*. Grand Rapids: Baker Academic, 1989.

Petersen, David L. *Zechariah 9–14 and Malachi*. Old Testament Library. Louisville, Ky.: Westminster John Knox, 1995.

Redditt, Paul L. *Haggai, Zechariah, Malachi*. The New Century Commentary. Grand Rapids: Eerdmans, 1995.

Reimer, David J. "צדק." Pages 744–69 in vol. 3 of *New International Dictionary of Old Testament Theology and Theology and Exegesis*. Edited by Willem A. VanGemeren. 5 vols. Grand Rapids: Zondervan, 1997.

Ringgren, Helmer. "בָּרָא." Pages 242–49 in vol. 2 of *Theological Dictionary of the Old Testament*. Rev. ed. Edited by G. Johannes Botterweck and Helmer Ringgren. Translated by John T. Willis. 15 vols. Grand Rapids: Eerdmans, 1977.

Rocine, B. M. *Learning Biblical Hebrew: A New Approach using Discourse Analysis*. Macon, Ga.: Smyth & Helwys, 2000.

Ross, Allen P. "שֵׁם." Pages 147–51 in vol. 4 of *New International Dictionary of Old Testament Theology and Exegesis*. Edited by Willem A. VanGemeren. 5 vols. Grand Rapids: Zondervan, 1997.

Scalise, Pamela J. "To Fear or Not to Fear: Questions of Reward and Punishment in Malachi 2:17–4:3." *Review and Expositor* 84, no. 3 (1987): 409–18.

Scharbert, Josef. "ארר." Pages 405–18 in vol. 1 of *Theological Dictionary of the Old Testament*. Edited by G. Johannes Botterweck. Translated by John T. Willis. 15 vols. Grand Rapids: Eerdmans, 1974.

Schoville, Keith N. "שׁמר." Pages 182–84 in vol. 4 of *New International Dictionary of Old Testament Theology and Exegesis*. Edited by Willem A. VanGemeren. 5 vols. Grand Rapids: Zondervan, 1997.

Schultz, Richard. "שׁפט." Pages 213–20 in vol. 4 of *New International*

Dictionary of Old Testament Theology and Exegesis. Edited by Willem A. VanGemeren. 5 vols. Grand Rapids: Zondervan, 1997.

Smith, John Merlin Powis, in Hinckley G. Mitchell, John M. P. Smith, and Julius A. Bewer. *A Critical and Exegetical Commentary on Haggai, Zechariah, Malachi, and Jonah.* The International Critical Commentary. Edinburgh: T&T Clark, 1912.

Smith, Ralph. *Micah–Malachi.* Word Biblical Commentary 32. Waco, Tex.: Word, 1984.

———. *Word Biblical Themes: Micah–Malachi.* Dallas: Word, 1990.

Stuart, Douglas. "Malachi." *The Minor Prophets: An Exegetical & Expository Commentary.* Vol. 3. Edited by Thomas Edward McComiskey. Grand Rapid: Baker, 1998.

Talley, David. "חפץ." Pages 231–34 in vol. 2 of *New International Dictionary of Old Testament Theology and Exegesis.* Edited by Willem A. VanGemeren. 5 vols. Grand Rapids: Zondervan, 1997.

Tate, Marvin E. "Questions for Priests and People in Malachi." *Review and Expositor* 84, no. 3 (1987): 391–407.

Thompson, David L. "יגע." Pages 400–402 in vol. 2 of *New International Dictionary of Old Testament Theology and Exegesis.* Edited by Willem A. VanGemeren. 5 vols. Grand Rapids: Zondervan, 1997.

Thompson, J. A., and Elmer A. Martens. "שׁוב." Pages 55–59 in vol. 4 of *New International Dictionary of Old Testament Theology and Exegesis.* Edited by Willem A. VanGemeren. 5 vols. Grand Rapids: Zondervan, 1997.

Van Dam, Cornelis. "הרס." Page 1061 in vol. 1 of *New International Dictionary of Old Testament Theology and Exegesis.* Edited by Willem A. VanGemeren. 5 vols. Grand Rapids: Zondervan, 1997.

———. "טרף." Pages 386–87 in vol. 2 of *New International Dictionary of Old Testament Theology and Exegesis.* Edited by Willem A. VanGemeren. 5 vols. Grand Rapids: Zondervan, 1997.

VanGemeren, Willem A., ed. *New International Dictionary of Old Testament Theology and Exegesis.* 5 vols. Grand Rapids: Zondervan, 1997.

Van Pelt, Miles V., and Walter C. Kaiser. "ירא." Pages 527–33 in vol.

2 of *New International Dictionary of Old Testament Theology and Exegesis*. Edited by Willem A. VanGemeren. 5 vols. Grand Rapids: Zondervan, 1997.

Verhoef, Pieter A. *The Books of Haggai and Malachi*. New International Commentary on the Old Testament. Grand Rapids: Eerdmans, 1987.

———. "יוֹם." Pages 419–24 in vol. 2 of *New International Dictionary of Old Testament Theology and Exegesis*. Edited by Willem A. VanGemeren. 5 vols. Grand Rapids: Zondervan, 1997.

Wakely, Robin. "בגד." Pages 582–95 in vol. 1 of *New International Dictionary of Old Testament Theology and Exegesis*. Edited by Willem A. VanGemeren. 5 vols. Grand Rapids: Zondervan, 1997.

Waltke, Bruce K., and Michael O'Connor. *An Introduction to Biblical Hebrew Syntax*. Winona Lake, Ind.: Eisenbrauns, 1990.

Watts, John D. W. "Introduction to the Book of Malachi." *Review and Expositor* 84, no. 3 (1987): 373–81.

Wendland, Ernst. "Linear and Concentric Patterns in Malachi." *The Bible Translator* 36, no. 1 (1985): 108–21.

Westermann, Claus. *Basic Forms of Prophetic Speech*. Translated by Hugh Clayton White. Louisville, Ky.: Westminster John Knox, 1991.

INDEX OF SCRIPTURE AND
OTHER ANCIENT SOURCES

Targum(s)		Vulgate	
Malachi		Malachi	
1:1	8	1:3	13
1:12	31	2:9	51
2:15	69	2:15	69
2:16	69	2:16	69, 71
2:17	74	2:17	74
3:8	92	3:8	92

AUTHOR INDEX

o186066

5486066

SUBJECT INDEX